CLASSIC HANDPLANES
AND JOINERY

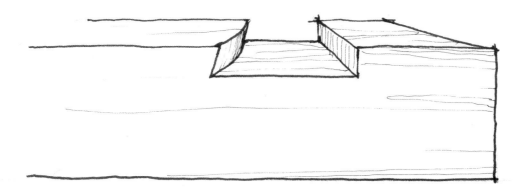

All art is by the author, except for the following: Figure 4-5 courtesy Lie-Nielsen Toolworks, Inc.; Figure 4-6 courtesy Veritas Tools, Inc.; Figure 4-8 courtesy Veritas Tools, Inc.; Figure 4-9 courtesy Stanley Black & Decker, Inc.; Figure 5-3 courtesy Veritas Tools, Inc.

ISBN 978-1-56523-962-3

Library of Congress Cataloging-in-Publication Data

Names: Wynn, Scott, author.
Title: Classic handplanes and joinery / Scott Wynn.
Description: Mount Joy : Fox Chapel Publishing, [2018] | Includes index.
Identifiers: LCCN 2018025435 (print) | LCCN 2018026341 (ebook) | ISBN
  9781607655381 (ebook) | ISBN 9781565239623
Subjects: LCSH: Joinery. | Woodwork.
Classification: LCC TH5662 (ebook) | LCC TH5662 .W96 2018 (print) | DDC
  694/.6--dc23
LC record available at https://lccn.loc.gov/2018025435

To learn more about the other great books from Fox Chapel Publishing, or to find a retailer near you, call toll-free
800-457-9112 or visit us at *www.FoxChapelPublishing.com*.

We are always looking for talented authors. To submit an idea, please send a brief inquiry to
acquisitions@foxchapelpublishing.com.

Printed in Singapore
First printing

CLASSIC HANDPLANES
AND JOINERY

Essential Tips and Techniques for Woodworkers

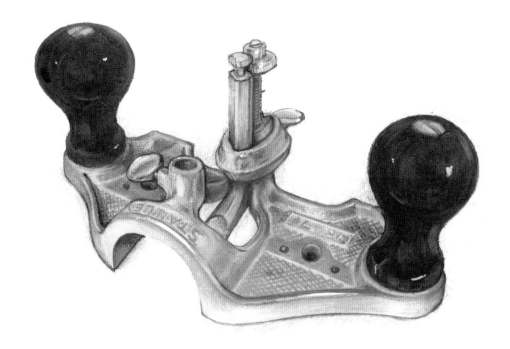

SCOTT WYNN

Fox Chapel
PUBLISHING

Contents

INTRODUCTION...................6

PART 1: THE BASICS

CHAPTER 1: STEEL..................9
Anatomy of Steel.................. 10
Types of Edge Steel................ 16

CHAPTER 2: UNDERSTANDING HOW
A PLANE WORKS 22
The Tactics....................23
The Angle of the Blade............24
Mouth Opening....................26
Chipbreaker....................28
Bevel Angle 29
Shape of the Blade Edge 30
Length of Plane/Width of Blade..30

CHAPTER 3: PLANE SETUP 32
Inspect the Plane....................33
Prepare the Blade 35
Prepare the Chipbreaker 41
Bed the Blade Properly............42
Configure the Sole 47
Check the Sole 49
Adjust the Mouth....................50

PART 2: THE PLANES

CHAPTER 4: RABBET PLANES 53
The Basic Rabbet Plane 54
Rabbet Bench and Block Planes 56
Skewed-Blade Rabbet Planes 57
The Stanley Rabbet Planes 58
Which One? 59
Using the Rabbet Plane 61
Setting Up Rabbet Planes 65

CHAPTER 5: FILLISTER AND
MOVING-FILLISTER PLANES 82
Choosing Your Fillister Plane.....85
Fence Solutions 86
Setting Up the
Moving-Fillister Plane 87
Using the Moving-Fillister
Plane 88

CHAPTER 6:
PLOUGH AND DADO PLANES........91
Using the Plough and Dado 95

CHAPTER 7: SHOULDER PLANES .96
Using the Shoulder Plane..........98

CHAPTER 8: BULLNOSE AND
CHISEL PLANES 100
Using Bullnose
and Chisel Planes 101

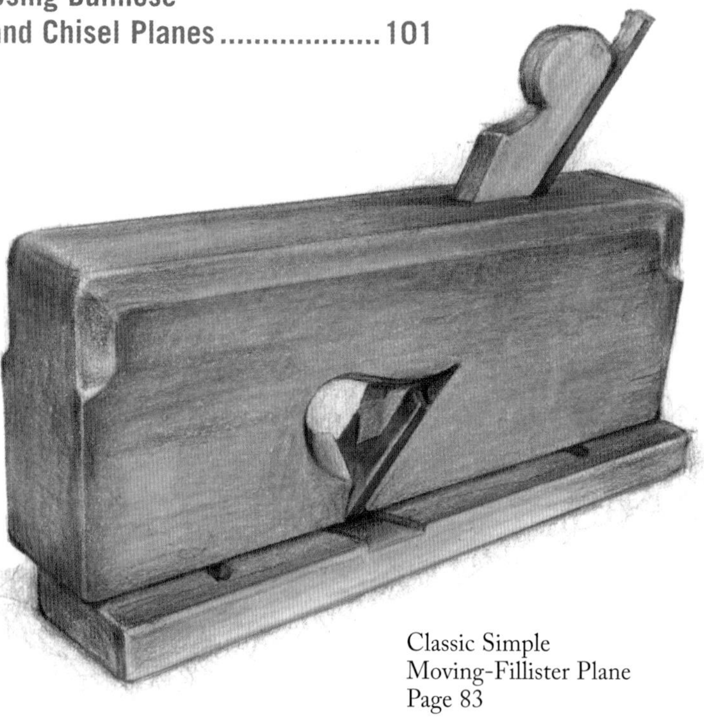

Classic Simple
Moving-Fillister Plane
Page 83

CHAPTER 9: THE ROUTER PLANE 103
The Stanley #71 Router Plane 105
Other Router Plane Options 113
Using the Router Plane 115

CHAPTER 10: SIDE-RABBET PLANES ... 116

CHAPTER 11: THE DOVETAIL PLANE 120

CHAPTER 12: THE MORTISE PLANE 124

PART 3: THE PROJECTS

CHAPTER 13:
MAKING A DOVETAIL PLANE 131
Creating the Plane 132
Making a Fence 133
Securing the Fence with Wedges 135

CHAPTER 14: MAKING AND USING
SHOOTING BOARDS 137
Designing a Shooting Board 138
Styles of Shooting Boards 139
Using a Shooting Board 142
The Dovetailed Stop 143

INDEX 157

Classic Traditional
Wood Plough Plane
Page 92

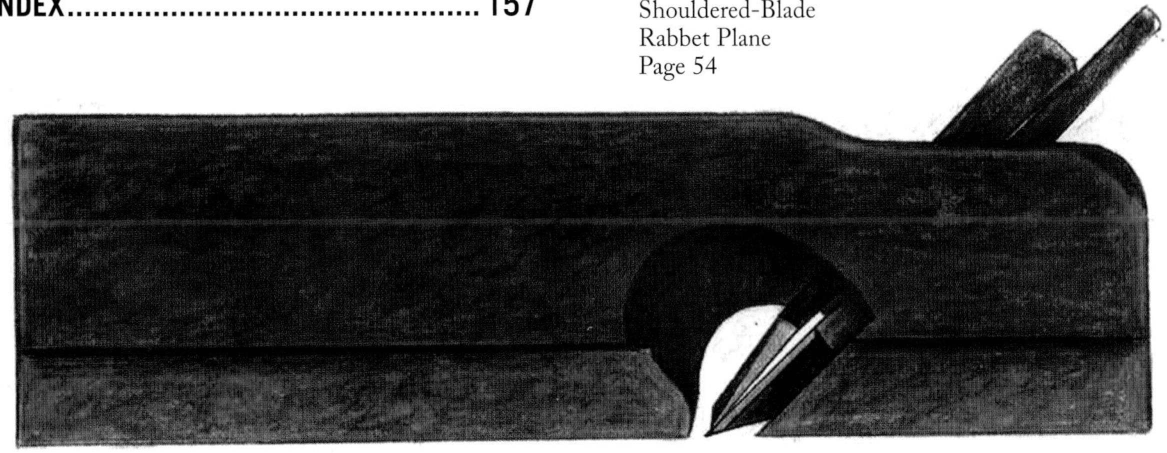

Typical Japanese
Shouldered-Blade
Rabbet Plane
Page 54

INTRODUCTION

The planes described in this book were originally created for making joints—grooves, rabbets, dovetails, and gains for hardware. We now usually use power tools to make these joints, but these planes remain irreplaceable. They can achieve a good fit on a wide variety of joints and also make joints that might otherwise be difficult or impossible with power machinery. These planes are so good at this that I believe they are indispensable for doing high-quality work.

For instance, say you cut a groove in a wide panel for a hardwood plywood partition. First of all, you can't use a ¾" (19mm) dado head on your table saw because hardwood plywood is less than ¾" (19mm) thick; it is ²³⁄₃₂" (18mm) thick, to be exact—except when it's not. Industry tolerances allow up to a ¹⁄₃₂" (0.8mm) variance in thickness, so some parts of your panel are thicker than others and your partition doesn't go into its slot. What do you do? Try to shift your router fence less than ¹⁄₃₂" (0.8mm) to try to get your specialty ²³⁄₃₂" (18mm) router bit to cut a bare fraction more? The easiest thing to do is make a pass or two with your side rabbet plane until that partition slides in. You can even use your side rabbet plane to only widen the groove in areas where the panel is thickest, so you don't end up with gaps along its length.

Sometimes you cut a groove in a panel or piece, and your partition goes in but not all the way; apparently the panel rode up slightly off the saw or router table top and the cut was not made full depth in some places. This is really common. If you run the piece over the table saw again, you run the risk of widening the cut. If you use your router plane, you can trim the dado to an exact depth for its entire length.

There are myriad uses for these planes that will get you a fine fit in a short amount of time. Sometimes these planes are not just the best option—they may be the only option for a good job.

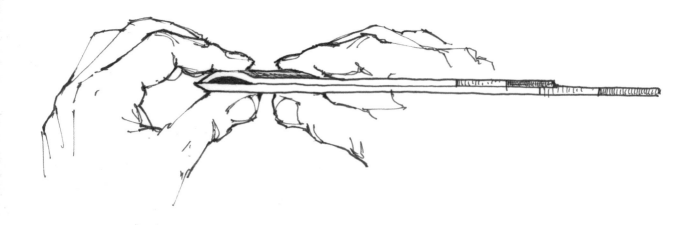

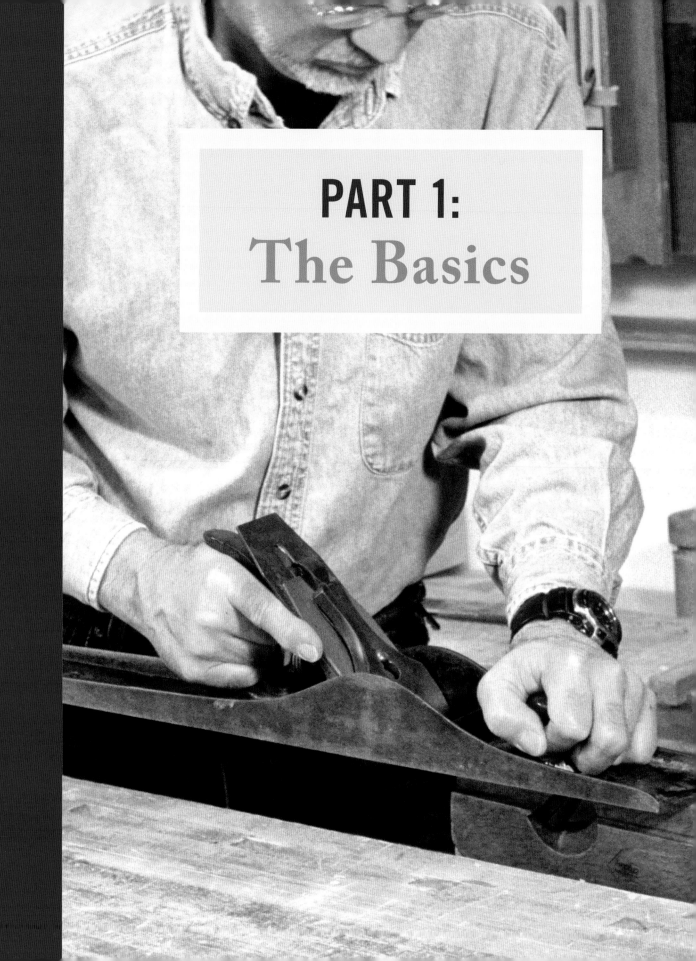

PART 1:
The Basics

1

Steel

As a woodworker it is really useful—perhaps mandatory—to know at least a little bit about blade steel. That bit of cutting edge is the direct extension of the image carried in your mind, shaping wood as you're visualizing it, constantly evaluating, re-analyzing, and revising in a feedback loop. This bit of cutting edge can work with you or it can be indifferent—or worse. Knowing what steel the blades in your planes are made of will help you understand that blade's abilities, limitations, and potential, how to best sharpen it, and, if you have the option, what might be the best steel for the kind of use to which you're putting the plane.

While with a joinery plane there may be few options beyond using the blade the plane came with, you can still sometimes find a few alternatives. You may be able to use a blade from a different period of manufacture as the manufacturer may have changed their steel over time; or a different manufacturer may have used a different steel at the same time period and the blade may be interchangeable. You could also be ambitious and make your own blades. And, for instance, some manufacturers, such as Veritas, now offer a choice of O1, A2, or PM-V11 steel for many of their blades.

Wait, wait . . . what is this alpha-numeric soup? Read on.

Anatomy of Steel

For the needs of the woodworker, three characteristics define steel's anatomy—grain, structure, and hardness.

Grain

For woodworking hand tools, the grain of the steel is the most important characteristic of a blade. Ordered, repetitive arrangements of iron and alloy atoms in a crystalline structure comprise steel. The crystals can be small and fine or large and coarse. They can be consistent in size (evenly grained) or vary widely, with odd shapes and outsized clusters in among the rest. The steel's grain affects how finely the blade sharpens and how quickly it dulls. Generally, the finer and more consistent the grain, the more finely a blade sharpens, the slower it dulls, and the better it performs.

Grain is a function of the initial quality of the steel used, the alloys added, and how the steel is worked or formed. In addition to the average size of the crystals, the initial quality of the steel may include impurities, called *inclusions*, which may persist throughout refining. Inclusions add large irregularities to the grain. Irregularities sometimes are used to good effect in swords and perhaps axes, but except for the backing steel on laminated blades, impurities are a detriment to a plane blade. Impurities, when sharpened out to the edge, break off easily, causing chipping and rapid dulling of the edge. The dirtier the steel, the more rapidly it dulls. Fine chipping will not affect the performance of an edge used for chopping wood; depending on the inclusion, it can add tensile, shock-resisting strength to the blade. But for fine woodworking, such as planing a surface, even fine inclusions prevent sharpening the blade to its full potential and shorten the edge's life.

Steel Grain

This standardized chart refers to the average grain size within a steel. The numbers range from 00 to 14, with 00 being the largest (about 1/50" [0.5mm]), and 14 the smallest (about 1/10000" [0.003mm]). Manufacturers normally use fine grain size 7 or finer for the steel used in tools.

ASTM Grain Size ASTM grain size number (N)	Average diameter of grain (assumed) as sphere at 1 X (mm)
00	0.51
0	0.36
1	0.25
2	0.18
3	0.125
4	0.090
5	0.065
6	0.045
7	0.032
8	0.022
9	0.016
10	0.011
11	0.008
12	0.006
13	0.004
14	0.003

From the article "Determining Austenite Grain Size of Steels: 4 Methods—Metallurgy" by Jayanti S., on *www.engineeringnotes.com.*

Alloys change the texture of the grain. They may be part of the steel's original composition (though usually in small amounts), or added in a recipe to increase the steel's resistance to shock and heat. Alloys often coarsen the grain, so there is a trade-off. While the edge of an alloy blade may be more durable, especially under adverse working conditions, it may not sharpen as well as an unalloyed blade. To shear wood cleanly, no other attribute of an edge is more important than fineness.

Structure

Structure, the second most important aspect of a woodworking blade, is the result of the change that happens in the original composition of the steel due to heating it and changing its shape with a hammer (or rollers), often called *hot work*. Heat causes the crystals of the steel to grow. Hammering steel when it is hot causes its crystalline structures to fracture and impedes growth as the grains fracture into smaller crystals. Before being hot-worked, the crystals of steel are randomly oriented and frequently inconsistent in size.

Through *forging* (repeatedly re-shaping with a hammer while the steel is hot), the grain aligns and knits together in the direction of the metal flow. Proper forging increases grain structure consistency. When exposed at the edge through sharpening, crystals consistent in size and orientation break off one at a time as the blade dulls, rather than

The Ideal Edge

The edge requirements for cutting different materials vary widely. The most obvious example is the edge required on a kitchen knife. Meat and vegetables are cut by the sawing action of drawing a coarse edge through them. A properly sharpened kitchen knife has what under a microscope would look like a series of small saw teeth, which result from sharpening it with an 800- or 1,200-grit stone. If you are skeptical, sharpen your best kitchen knife like a plane blade with a #8000 stone and try to cut a potato. It will stop cutting halfway through and jam: the knife is sharp enough to cut transparent shavings in wood, but it will not cut halfway through a root vegetable.

Shaving is another one: a razor is somewhat coarsely sharpened so its edge is a series of fine teeth. These "teeth" are then polished with a very fine stone and strop. The teeth snag the hairs and the polish on the teeth allows them to cut the hair. It should be sharper for good woodworking. The lesson is that demonstrations of sharpness using other materials and claims of qualities originating in other trades and uses, such as industry or surgery, are not particularly useful in evaluating a woodworking blade.

Conceptually, for a blade to be perfect for woodworking, it must be possible to polish it down to single-crystal uniformity across its entire edge, with the crystals all lined up neatly, oriented the same direction, all very small and of the same size, equally hard, and tightly bonded to one another so they will not break off. In reality, several types of crystals comprise a cutting edge. The crystals are greatly different in size and hardness and grouped together so they present themselves at the cutting edge in clusters, and so tend to break off in clusters, leaving voids and dull spots. The finest blades, however, have the qualities that enable something approaching the ideal edge.

breaking off randomly in big clumps. The consistency of the crystals allows for a sharper blade that stays sharp longer.

The techniques used in preparing steel for woodworking tools are hammer forging, drop forging, and no forging. *Hammer forging*, where repeated hammer blows shape the steel, is the most desirable because it aligns the grain particles (or crystals) of the steel. It is a time-consuming, skillful process and therefore expensive. If improperly done, hammer forging stresses the steel, reducing, rather than increasing, reliability. With the general decline in hand-woodworking skills during the last century, and the increased reliance on power tools, the discriminating market that would appreciate the difference forging makes has shrunk considerably. As a result, hand-forged tools are not commonly manufactured or available in the United States.

Drop forging verges on die cutting. A large, mechanized hammer called the punch drops on the heated blank, smashing it into a die (mold), giving the tool blade its rough shape, often in just one blow. For tools that vary considerably in cross section, this method may be more desirable than grinding or cutting from stock, because the heat of grinding or cutting can cause some minor negative alteration in the grain structure at those areas. Drop forging imparts a marginally more consistent structure than a blade cut or ground from stock. The steel often elongates in the process, resulting in some improvement in the crystalline structure alignment.

Drop forging is preferable to *no forging* at all, though no forging is an over-simplification, because all tool steel receives some hot work during reshaping. Bar stock is hot-formed by rolling or extruding the ingot into lengths of consistent cross section. The process rearranges the crystalline structure, and the crystals tend to align in the direction of the flow as the steel lengthens. However, the arrangement is not very refined compared with the structure resulting when steel is hot-worked more at the forge. Modern Western chisel blades are frequently drop-forged (though some new premium chisels are being ground from A2 bar stock). Modern Western plane blades, even many after-market premium blades, are usually ground from unworked, rolled stock.

Hardness

Hardness is a major selling point in the advertising of woodworking tools made from various types of steel. However, as explained earlier, grain and structure are the most important factors in the performance of a blade. A plane blade soft enough to shape with a file (for instance, made from a piece of a good, old handsaw blade) will give excellent results if the fineness of its grain allows it to be sharpened well and its structure allows the edge to break off finely and evenly. I knew a boat builder who preferred plane blades made from

Hardening, Tempering, and Annealing

Steel's hardness and ductility (the extent to which it can be stretched or bent without breaking) depends on its exact carbon-to-iron ratio and its thermal processing. Different temperatures are associated with different crystal structures, or phases, of the iron and carbon atoms. When steel with a carbon content above 0.4% (the minimum amount required for steel to harden) is heated beyond its critical temperature of around 750°C, it enters what is called the *austenite phase*. Austenite has a crystal structure that opens to allow the carbon atoms present to combine with the iron.

When austenite is cooled very quickly (by quenching), its structure changes to a needlelike crystalline form called *martensite*. Martensite locks in the carbon atom, *hardening* the steel. In this state, the steel is at its hardest, is under a great deal of internal stress, and is quite brittle. The more carbon the steel had to begin with, the more of it will be martensite and the harder it will be. As the carbon goes over 0.8%, however, the steel does not become any harder, but rather grows more brittle. In order for the steel to be useable as a blade, it must be softened to reduce the brittleness to a workable degree. This process is called *tempering*.

Tempering is a compromise, meant to balance hardness and ductility, and is definitely a judgment call made by the one doing the tempering, based both on experience and the intended use of the blade. To temper a blade, after hardening, the blade is reheated, this time to a lower temperature, perhaps 175°C (depending on the type of steel and the blade's intended use), and quenched again.

There is a third process, done after the blade has been hot-worked to shape, but before hardening and tempering, and that is *annealing*. Here the blade is heated red-hot and allowed to cool *without* quenching. This softens the blade and removes stresses that may have resulted from its being hot-worked. Usually at this point, the blade is then ground to final (or near final) shape—easily done, since it is now soft—and then hardened and finally tempered.

high-quality saw blades. The blades made it easy for him to file out nicks when his plane hit unexpected metal in the boat structure.

At the other end of the hardness spectrum is carbide, used on power tool blades. Hard and brittle, carbide is unsuitable for the body of the tool blade because it would shatter. While carbide is extremely hard, the particles are also extremely large. Although they do not break off easily, when they do, they break off in clumps so big they are nearly visible to the naked eye. Carbide also cannot be made nearly as sharp as steel. A sharp steel saw or router blade cuts much more cleanly than a sharp carbide blade. Unfortunately, the steel dulls quicker than the carbide, especially when subjected to the glues in plywood and particleboard.

Hardness must be in balance with the intended use of the tool. For instance, high-impact hand tools, such as axes,

ROCKWELL HARDNESS SCALES

	Scale Symbol	Indenter Type (Ball dimensions indicate diameter.)	Preliminary Force N* (kgf**)	Total Force N (kgf)	Typical Applications
Regular Rockwell Scales	A	Spheroconical Diamond	98.07 (10)	588.4 (60)	Cemented carbides, thin steel, and shallow case hardened steel.
	B	Ball - 1/16" (1.588mm)	98.07 (10)	980.7 (100)	Copper alloys, soft steels, aluminum alloys, malleable iron, etc.
	C	Spheroconical Diamond	98.07 (10)	1471 (150)	Steel, hard cast irons, pearlitic malleable iron, titanium, deep case hardened steel, and other materials harder than HRB 100.
	D	Spheroconical Diamond	98.07 (10)	980.7 (100)	Thin steel and medium case hardened steel, and pearlitic malleable iron.
	E	Ball - 1/8" (3.175mm)	98.07 (10)	980.7 (100)	Cast iron, aluminum and magnesium alloys, and bearing metals.
	F	Ball - 1/16" (1.588mm)	98.07 (10)	588.4 (60)	Annealed copper alloys, and thin soft sheet metals.
	G	Ball - 1/16" (1.588mm)	98.07 (10)	1471 (150)	Malleable irons, copper-nickel-zinc, and cupro-nickel alloys.
	H	Ball - 1/8" (3.175mm)	98.07 (10)	588.4 (60)	Aluminum, zinc, and lead.
	K	Ball - 1/8" (3.175mm)	98.07 (10)	1471 (150)	Bearing metals and other very soft or thin materials. Use smallest ball and heaviest load that does not give anvil effect.
	L	Ball - 1/4" (6.350mm)	98.07 (10)	588.4 (60)	
	M	Ball - 1/4" (6.350mm)	98.07 (10)	980.7 (100)	
	P	Ball - 1/4" (6.350mm)	98.07 (10)	1471 (150)	
	R	Ball - 1/2" (12.70mm)	98.07 (10)	588.4 (60)	
	S	Ball - 1/2" (12.70mm)	98.07 (10)	980.7 (100)	
	V	Ball - 1/2" (12.70mm)	98.07 (10)	1471 (150)	

* N, or newton, is the international unit of force named after Sir Isaac Newton. To move an object with a mass of 1 kilogram meter per second per second, 1 newton of force is needed.

** kgf, or kilogram-force, is the gravitational metric unit of force. At Earth's surface, 1 kilogram-force is the force of gravity on a mass of 1 kilogram. Gravity accelerates any object at 9.8 meters per second per second, so 1 kilogram-force is equal to 9.8 newtons.

From *Rockwell Hardness Measurement of Metallic Materials* by Samuel R. Low, published by the National Institute of Standards and Technology, U.S. Department of Commerce

		ROCKWELL HARDNESS SCALES *(CONTINUED)*			
Superficial Rockwell Scales	15N	Spheroconical Diamond	29.42 (3)	147.1 (15)	Similar to A, C, and D scales, but for thinner gage material or case depth.
	30N	Spheroconical Diamond	29.42 (3)	294.2 (30)	
	45N	Spheroconical Diamond	29.42 (3)	441.3 (45)	
	15T	Ball - ¹⁄₁₆″ (1.588mm)	29.42 (3)	147.1 (15)	Similar to B, F, and G scales, but for thinner gage material.
	30T	Ball - ¹⁄₁₆″ (1.588mm)	29.42 (3)	294.2 (30)	
	45T	Ball - ¹⁄₁₆″ (1.588mm)	29.42 (3)	441.3 (45)	
	15W	Ball - ⅛″ (3.175mm)	29.42 (3)	147.1 (15)	Very soft material.
	30W	Ball - ⅛″ (3.175mm)	29.42 (3)	294.2 (30)	
	45W	Ball - ⅛″ (3.175mm)	29.42 (3)	441.3 (45)	
	15X	Ball - ¼″ (6.350mm)	29.42 (3)	147.1 (15)	
	30X	Ball - ¼″ (6.350mm)	29.42 (3)	294.2 (30)	
	45X	Ball - ¼″ (6.350mm)	29.42 (3)	441.3 (45)	
	15Y	Ball - ½″ (12.70mm)	29.42 (3)	147.1 (15)	
	30Y	Ball - ½″ (12.70mm)	29.42 (3)	294.2 (30)	
	45Y	Ball - ½″ (12.70mm)	29.42 (3)	441.3 (45)	

From *Rockwell Hardness Measurement of Metallic Materials* by Samuel R. Low, published by the National Institute of Standards and Technology, U.S. Department of Commerce

should be softer than plane blades. Otherwise, the edge fractures quickly under the pounding an ax takes. The blades of fine tools for fine work can be very hard, but if their hardness exceeds the ability of the steel to flex without breaking at the microscopic edge, the tool will be next to worthless.

The *Rockwell C (Rc)* scale measures the hardness of woodworking blades. This is a unit of measurement determined by the impact of a ball-shaped point into the steel measured in terms of the depth of the resulting impression. The steel in a common grade of handsaw measures around 46–48 Rc, with high-quality Disston saws (at their peak when Disston still owned them) measuring 52–54 Rc. Harder yet, Japanese saws are roughly in the 50–58 Rc range; this is on the cusp of what a file will cut. Decent plane and chisel blades are in the range of 58–66 Rc range—though I would expect a good quality plane blade to be at least 60–62 Rc. Only some finely wrought steels work effectively in the upper-half of this range, principally high-quality hand-forged Japanese blades, and some high-alloy steels. In carbon steels, 66 Rc seems to

FIGURE 1-1. The polished bevel on a cast steel blade reveals the lamination of the backing steel and the cast steel; the color difference is where the two are forge-welded together.

FIGURE 1-2. The color line on the back of this old unpolished rabbet plane blade shows right where the piece of cast steel leaves off and the backing steel takes over for the rest of the blade.

be a limit above which the edge breaks down too rapidly in use.

Types of Edge Steel

Steel for hand tool blades can be roughly divided into two categories: carbon steel and alloyed steel. All tool steels contain carbon, which is what makes it possible to harden the metal. Processed from iron and iron ore, carbon steel contains at least 0.5% carbon, and traces of other elements. Alloyed steel is carbon steel with small amounts of other elements added to improve performance under certain conditions and for certain purposes.

Although manufacturers of steel have specific guidelines with regard to the percentages of alloys used in their steels, and each recipe is identified with a name, manufacturers of woodworking tools, at least until recently, usually chose to ignore the nomenclature. They instead choose to give a broadly descriptive or generic term for the steel that may encompass many different steels of widely varying recipes and characteristics, based on how they perceived the market. One example of a descriptive term like this is "tungsten vanadium." As it turns out, there are quite a few steels with tungsten and vanadium, each widely varying in their percentage—and performance characteristics. This is in direct contrast to contemporary knife makers who are

Alloy Ingredients

Carbon added to iron makes it harder and more wear-resistant. Carbon content of about 0.5% to 0.6% is about the lowest amount found in tool steel. The low-carbon steel is used for hammers, blacksmith tools, etc. A carbon content of about 0.8% makes a steel file hard (about 56–58 Rc). Carbon above that level does not increase the steel's hardness, but raises its wear resistance. A carbon content of 1.3% is about the highest. The highest-carbon steel is used for razors, engraving tools, etc. A carbon content of about 1.05% is a good average—hard with good wear resistance, and yet not fussy or sensitive to heat.

Tungsten, added in small quantities, can impart a tight, small, and dense grain structure and the ability to attain a keen cutting edge. It also enables steel to retain its hardness at higher temperatures and has a detrimental effect on the steel's forgeability. A tungsten content of 4% (with 1.3% carbon) is so hard that it is difficult to grind with an emery wheel.

Manganese makes steel sound when first cast into ingots, and easier to hot roll or forge. Practically all tool steel has at least 0.2% of manganese. Steel can contain up to 0.5% manganese before it is considered alloy steel.

Silicon facilitates casting and hot work. It usually is used in combination with manganese, molybdenum, or chromium. All steel has 0.1% to 0.3% silicon. Steel with 0.5% to 2% silicon content is considered an alloy.

Chromium increases the hardness penetration of the steel. A thick bar of plain carbon steel will be hardened to a depth of only ¾₆" (5mm) from its face during heat treatment. Adding chromium allows the bar to harden all the way through. Because most woodworking blades are less than ⅜" (9mm) thick, it is not really an issue for woodworkers. Chromium increases the steel's wear resistance under impact and heat, but does not necessarily increase its hardness. Steel with chromium content of 4% and higher is called high-speed steel.

quite specific about which steel they are using in their blades, such as 12C27, 9Cr13CoMoV, or 440C. Recently, hand tool makers have been a little more specific about what type of steel they use for their blades, such as O-1 and A-2, but this is by no means consistent. If you already have a plane and want to know what kind of steel the blade is, you can put it on the grinder and look up the resulting spark pattern; this will give you a good indication of its general type. Of course, you can also use it and see if it performs as you want it to, in which case it may not make any difference what type it is. If you're buying or replacing a blade, the following information should help.

When manufactured properly, carbon steel sharpens optimally, holds a sharp edge, and re-sharpens easily—the three basic requirements of a woodworking blade. Its manufacture can be varied slightly to accommodate different woodworking tasks. Many variations exist, based mostly on the quality of ingredients and manufacture, how much it had been hot-worked, and what incidental alloys may be included.

Type	Pros	Cons
White steel	• A forged, very hard, and serviceable Japanese steel capable of getting and keeping a very keen edge, making it ideal for use in difficult-to-plane softwoods and most hardwoods	• While white steel's long, angular grain structure allows it to take a very keen edge (keener than blue steel), it is less durable in use with abrasive woods than its blue steel cousin
Blue steel	• Both blue steel and white steel get their names from the wrapping paper the mill uses to identify the two. Also forged, blue steel has an addition of tungsten, making it more serviceable in hard and abrasive woods	• Even more expensive than white steel
Cast steel	• A forged, very pure steel • High quality and highly predictable • Takes and holds an edge ideally suited to woodworking	• No longer manufactured • Like blue steel and white steel, the blades always need to be forge-welded (laminated) to a softer, more tensile steel
"Plain" carbon steel	• Very serviceable, but undistinguished blades, unless forged • Easy to shape and harden • Perfect for making specific blades for specific tools; try one of the 10xx steels, such as 1095	• Quite a bit of variation in quality, which can be hard to identify until the blade is used • Usually manufactured with unworked bar stock

ALLOY STEEL

An allow steel allows a blade to imitate some of the qualities of a good hand-worked carbon blade without the cost of handwork—with generally limited success. Generally, they are particularly suited for hard-use conditions. While they may not get as keen an edge as a finely wrought carbon-steel blade, their capacity for keeping their edge is excellent. As a result, they are a viable choice for joint-forming planes (as opposed to joint-trimming planes) where the stress and heat of deep, repetitive cuts and impact all take a toll on the edge (**Figure 1-3**).

Alloyed steels require different sharpening methods, increasingly so as the alloy content grows. The greater the alloy content, the less effective are water and oilstones, necessitating a diamond stone or paste. The technique and the amount of time is about the same, though, once the different abrasives are employed. Each alloy type has its own advantages and pitfalls. Read on to learn more.

Type	Pros	Cons
Chrome and tungsten vanadium	• These blades are workhorses and very durable • Well suited to general, heavy work • Great for many miscellaneous tasks around the shop • Recommended for forming work	• Since they are coarser grained, they are not suited for making fine, tearout-free shavings in many woods
PM-V11	• Consistent grain size • Great durability • Easy to sharpen • An all-around blade steel • Recommended for joint forming and trimming • Handy when the wood gets harder and blade angle higher when A2 is no longer sufficient when fine tuning	• There is tougher steel available, and ones that can be made sharper
D2/M2	• Extremely durable edge • Suitable for high impact, abrasion, and high temperatures	• With the possible exception of high-angle blades used with tropical hardwoods, its coarse grain structure makes it unsuitable for most plane blades

A2	• Affordable quality and highly consistent content • Finer grained than chrome and tungsten vanadium • High performance across a spectrum of tasks and difficult woods • Recommended for forming and trimming work	• Method of sharpening depends on the manufacturer; some may be sharpened with waterstones, while others may require diamond stones • Not ideal for stock removal
O1	• Shows greater endurance in shaping tasks than carbon steel • Easy to sharpen • Takes a keener edge than A2 • Good choice for trimming	• Not as durable as A2
High-speed steel (HSS)	• Its durability is ideally suited for very high blade-angle planes (60° or above) such as a rabbet plane used on tropical hardwoods	• Not recommended for general use in planing • Impossible to hone on more common sharpening stones (diamond stone or paste are needed for sharpening) • Doesn't get as sharp as carbon or other alloy steels • Has a coarser grain than other alloy steels, so it has limitations

FIGURE 1-3. This dovetail plane uses a chrome vanadium blade.

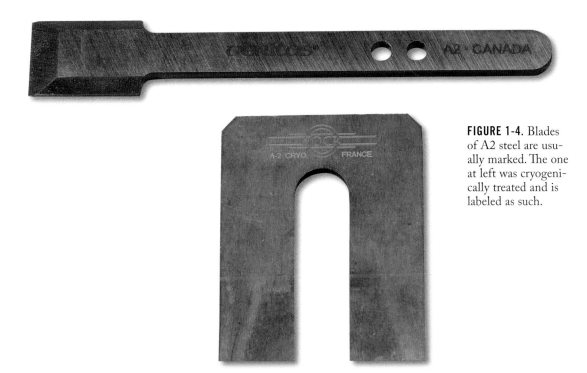

FIGURE 1-4. Blades of A2 steel are usually marked. The one at left was cryogenically treated and is labeled as such.

2

Understanding How a Plane Works

The Tactics

All planes, not just bench planes, use these same "tactics" to achieve the performance they were designed for. While often built in, especially on joinery planes, there are ways to vary the tactics both individually and in groups to improve performance.

1. **Angle of the blade to the work**. You will notice with the joinery planes that the blade angles can vary considerably from one type of plane to another.

2. **Clearance of the mouth through which the shaving passes**. Some of the joinery planes have no mouth, or even a "sole" sometimes; others have very tight mouths, or adjustable mouths.

3. **The use of a chipbreaker.** A relatively recent invention that nearly eliminates tearout while increasing a plane's versatility, though many joinery planes don't have one.

4. **Angle of the blade's bevel**. Not having the correct blade bevel angle causes many headaches.

5. **Shape of the blade edge.** Unlike bench planes, almost all joinery planes have blades sharpened straight across, though they might have other edges shaped or sharpened.

6. **Length of the plane body and width of the blade.** Since joinery planes are not used for preparing stock, there is a surprising similarity in size across most woodworking cultures. Knowing a bit about why planes vary in length and width may help you solve problems.

Cutting End Grain

End grain is best cut at the lowest possible angle: in practice about 22°—or about the size of the bevel of a paring chisel—which works quite well for shearing end grain, but is hard to control. The traditional solution, rather than using a blade, was to mount a blade in a plane at a low angle (12° to 18°) with the bevel up. The arrangement, somewhat compromising of performance on end grain, gains the advantages of control, adjustability, jigging (provided by the sole of the plane), and the ability to plane end grain with some reliability.

Many planes are set up like this, such as the Stanley 60-½, which can be used on a shooting board to plane board ends, as well as to perform the multitude of other tasks. Another plane of note was the Stanley 62 low-angle jack plane (now remade by Lie-Nielsen and Veritas). Shoulder planes, a joint-making plane discussed in Chapter 7, page 96, were developed mainly from a need to even out the end grain of poorly cut tenon shoulders.

The Angle of the Blade

To be more accurate, the *angle of the blade* should be called the *angle of the cutting edge*. It is the angle at which the cutting edge is presented to the work. On blades with the bevel down toward the work, it is the angle of the blade as positioned in the plane, sometimes called the bedding angle. On blades with the bevel up, it is the bedding angle plus the angle of the bevel (**Figure 2-1**).

The correct cutting angle for the species of wood being worked can help reduce tearout, though by itself it will not always eliminate it.

The angle of the cut ideally should vary according to the wood being worked. Softer woods take a lower cutting angle than hard woods, 37°–45°. So, the harder the wood, the higher the cutting angle, from 47.5° to 60° for northern hardwoods. Also, end grain cuts differently than long grain, cutting best

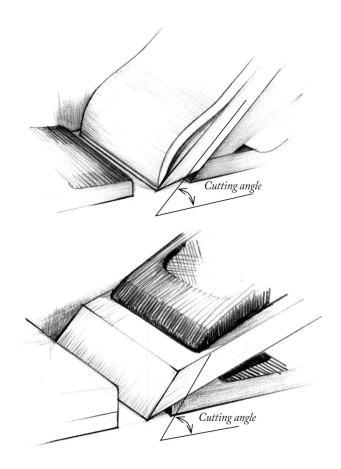

Cutting angle

Cutting angle

FIGURE 2-1. The cutting angle is the angle that the cutting edge presents to the work. On blades with the bevel down (top), it is the angle of the blade in the plane (the bedding angle). On blades with the bevel up, it is the angle of the blade in the plane plus the angle of the bevel (bottom).

Pitch Angles

While Western blade angles are usually measured in degrees, the pitch of a Japanese plane blade is determined using a rise/run scale based on 10 rather than degrees. That is why you will sometimes come across such apparently odd pitches as 47½°, which is actually a rise of 11 in a run of 10. Curiously, these pitches can also be found in English planes. Norris planes often had a pitch of 47½°, and I have an American razee try plane with a 43° blade angle (a 9 in 10 pitch). These are my favorite blade angles for smoothing wood; 43° does a nice job on many of the softer hardwoods, as well as maple, and 47½° works well on many of the harder hardwoods. The latter pitch also seems to be a critical angle around which the geometry of the cut begins to change.

FIGURE 2-2. Blade Angle and Wood Species.
Within the range for each wood, the lower angles are generally for preparatory planes. The higher angles are for smoothing planes.

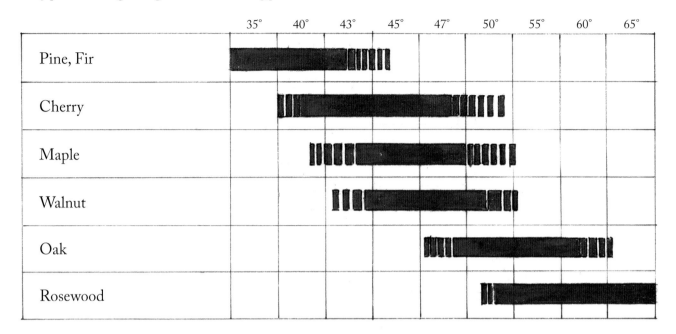

	35°	40°	43°	45°	47°	50°	55°	60°	65°
Pine, Fir									
Cherry									
Maple									
Walnut									
Oak									
Rosewood									

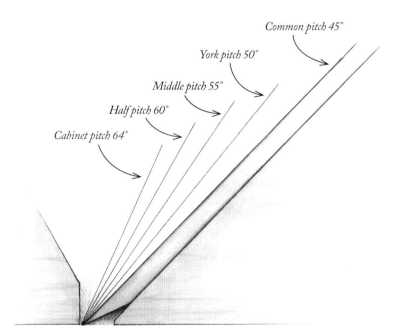

Common pitch 45°

York pitch 50°

Middle pitch 55°

Half pitch 60°

Cabinet pitch 64°

FIGURE 2-3. British nomenclature for common blade angles (pitch).

at a very low angle, 40° or less (**Figure 2-2**). Traditional blade angles for tropical hardwoods often are quite high, 60° or more. Despite the high angle, the plane blade leaves a clean-cut surface with good clarity on these woods (**Figure 2-3**).

Rabbet, fillister, plough, and dado planes often have their blades bedded at 45° or lower (though antique wood bodied planes can often be found with higher angles, and Chinese and Australian planes can be found with cutting angles of 60°). This 45° angle can be a problem for use in the harder

FIGURE 2-4. Here you can see the traditional use of different blade angles according to the work. The plane in front is a plane used for forming rounds for moldings, with a blade angle of 55°. Behind that is a rabbet plane used for both trimming and forming rabbets with a blade angle of 47.5° (a surprisingly common angle often used on intermediate planes for hardwood). Behind them all is a Stanley #6 Foreplane, usually used as a preliminary, roughing plane with a blade angle of 45°.

woods, especially tropical hardwood and figured woods (**Figure 2-4**).

If you need to work on tropical hardwoods, or you need to improve the cut of a plane used to trim and smooth a joint, there are two ways you can increase the cutting angle of the blade. One way is to alter the angle of the bevel on the blade itself in planes with the bevel of the blade mounted up. Because the bevel is mounted up, any change in its angle changes the cutting angle. The disadvantage is that increasing the bevel angle often results in an angle blunter than normally desirable, cutting action is reduced, the edge may dull quicker (it was blunter to begin with), and the plane requires greater effort to push.

In planes with the bevel mounted down, you can back-bevel a blade. This is where you put a second bevel on the topside of the blade, opposite to the main bevel. This is usually a small bevel established by honing rather than by grinding. For instance, if your bevel-down blade is bedded at 45° and you think you could get a better cut with a 55° angle, you can put a 10° angle on the back (top) of the blade: 45° + 10° = 55°.

Unfortunately, the downside of this is that if you want to restore the original cutting angle, you have to grind away the depth of the back bevel to restore the original edge, which is a loss of blade length—and time. However, back-beveling can be an effective solution for those occasional situations.

A surprising amount of tearout at any angle is avoided by having an extremely sharp blade. Get the blade as sharp as you can and keep it that way.

Mouth Opening

Controlling the shaving as it passes through the opening in the bottom of the plane is probably the second most basic technique for controlling tearout. Restricting the mouth opening works to reduce tearout (**Figure 2-5**) by compressing the wood fibers immediately in front of the blade. This keeps them from splitting out ahead of the cut (**Figure 2-6**).

The option of controlling the chip by use of a fine mouth opening is, however, not available on most of the joinery planes. The router plane is the most obvious example of this. Plough planes don't even have what could be called a sole (let alone a mouth); rather, it is a narrow piece of steel (called a skate) barely ⅛" (3mm) wide, much narrower than the narrowest blade usually used.

However, modern bench and block plane-style rabbet and fillister planes now have adjustable mouths, as do good-quality shoulder planes. This tactic can be quite effective for reducing or even eliminating tearout. The trick is not to make the mouth smaller than the thickness of the shaving that has to pass through it, but only very slightly larger (**Figure 2-7**). This is easy to misjudge, and can be frustrating. If the mouth is too small for the cut, the shavings jam in the throat. This can damage the edge of the mouth and sometimes the blade. Restricting the chip at the mouth of the plane definitely increases stress on the blade, as both pressure and heat build. The increased downward pressure on the blade due to the chip being constricted as it passes through the mouth increases the importance of the correct bevel angle, as the blade edge is liable to flex (see "Bevel Angle" on page 29). When this happens, it flexes deeper into the cut, taking a slightly thicker chip (**Figure 2-8**). The result is one of three things: tearout, a chattering cut (as the blade flexes back and forth), or a chip too large for the opening, which causes the chip to jam.

Closing the mouth down also increases the wear on the edge of the mouth itself. For maximum effectiveness, the edge of the mouth should be crisp.

FIGURE 2-5. Un-restrained shaving splits out ahead of cut, causing tearout.

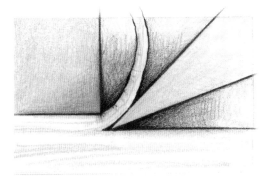

FIGURE 2-6. Shaving restrained by a tight mouth opening prevents shaving from lifting ahead of the cut, reducing or eliminating tearout.

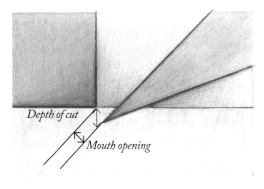

Depth of cut

Mouth opening

FIGURE 2-7. For maximum effectiveness against tearout, the mouth opening is equal to the depth of cut. In the real world, the mouth may have to be ever so slightly larger, but definitely no less than, the depth of cut.

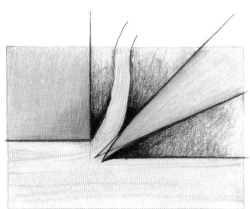

FIGURE 2-8. A mouth opening or bevel angle that is too small can cause the edge to flex.

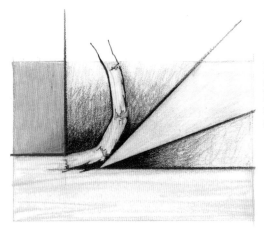

FIGURE 2-9. As the shaving rides up the blade, it can lift and split out ahead of the cut.

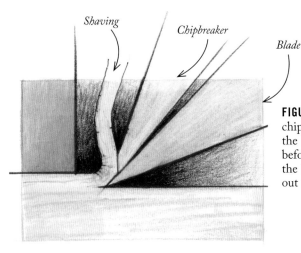

Shaving

Chipbreaker

Blade

FIGURE 2-10. The chipbreaker breaks the shaving (chip) before it can ride up the blade and split out ahead of the cut.

Sharp is even better. The increased pressure from constricting the chip eventually rounds the edge over. The rounder it gets, the less effective it is.

Increased heat buildup at the mouth is palpable. The oils in the wood being planed vaporize and condense on the top edge of the blade, causing a superficial discoloration of the blade just above the edge. Sometimes when you disassemble a blade to sharpen it, you will see evidence of this discoloration on the top of the blade.

Chipbreaker

The chipbreaker is a 300- to 400-year-old invention that has increased the reliability of the handplane in getting consistently smooth results. The chipbreaker accomplishes this through a tactic that gives the piece its name: by sharpening the bevel on the chipbreaker and placing it directly behind the cutting edge (**Figure 2-9**) the chip is broken before it has a chance to lift and split ahead of the cut (**Figure 2-10**). This has proven to be a highly effective method of reducing tearout, especially when coupled with a small mouth opening at lower-to-medium blade angles. Some designs also help stiffen a blade, giving it more stability.

The chipbreaker should be honed as keen and smooth as the blade, mated perfectly to the blade. The angle of its bevel plus that of the blade should equal around 90° to 100° relative to the sole of the plane.

How close should the chipbreaker be set to the edge? Generally, the chipbreaker is set back from the edge in a distance equal to the maximum thickness of the shaving you expect to make with that plane. For the finest finish work, I set the chipbreaker down until there is only the barest glint of light left on the top (back) of the blade. This is much less than 1/64" (0.4mm) because only that fine line of light tells me there is still some blade exposed. For the adjustment to work, the chipbreaker must be very well prepared (see "Prepare the Chipbreaker" on page 41), or the chips will jam.

For coarse work, the chipbreaker can be set well back, though it is usually not necessary to set it back much more than ¹⁄₁₆" (2mm).

Bevel Angle

The bevel angle is the angle to which the blade is sharpened. Most blades leave the factory with a 25° or 30° bevel angle. To bring a plane to its finest performance, the bevel angle may well need further attention (**Figure 2-11**).

If the bevel angle is too small, the edge flexes under the load, bending down until the chip releases, and then springing up to its original position. It may do this repeatedly, resulting in chatter. Or, the edge may flex under the stress of cutting the shaving, especially if it hits a harder part of the board, diving down into the wood and cutting a chip thicker than it was set for. If the plane has a very fine mouth, the thicker chip may jam the mouth instead of springing back up. Or, the edge can flex under the chipbreaker, opening a gap between the two, which will jam with chips. Therefore, even though the rest of the plane is otherwise finely tuned, the mouth can continue to jam.

As a rule of thumb, the bevel angle should be as small as will cut without chattering. Larger angles and a restricted mouth opening will place increased stress on the blade edge, causing it to

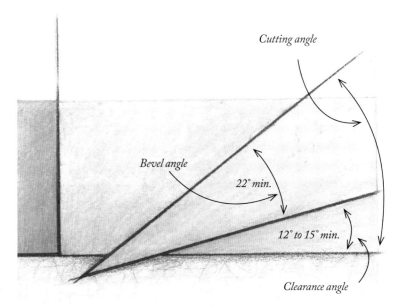

FIGURE 2-11. Practical minimum bevel angle and clearance angle.

The Correct Bevel Angle

There are limits and ranges you can use as rules of thumb in correcting the bevel angle. First, the minimum clearance angle on a bevel-down blade should be about 12°, though 15° would be better. The parameter will limit the size of the bevel angle on low-angle planes. For instance, if you have a plane with a 35°-cutting angle, the bevel angle of the blade is going to be limited to a maximum of 23° (35° - 12° = 23°). The practical lower limit of the bevel for most blades is about 22°—any smaller and the blade usually crumples at the edge in common use. And some blade steels such as A2 may have trouble giving good service at such a small bevel angle. Also, the bevel angle varies according to the bedding angle of the blade; the steeper the bedding angle, the greater the bevel angle should be. For instance, a plane with a bedding angle of 40° could have a bevel angle of 22°; 25° to 28° would probably be more serviceable; a 45° plane would have a bevel angle of 25° to 30°. A plane with a bedding angle of 55° could have a bevel angle of 30° to 32°, to perhaps as much as 35°. A bedding angle of 65° could have a bevel angle of as much as 38° to 40°.

deflect in use. Increasing the bevel angle will alleviate this. The objective is to increase the bevel angle only enough to eliminate chattering. Any more increases resistance and may reduce the smoothness of the cut. Begin with the factory angle and see how it performs. If you suspect it is too small, then increase the bevel angle until you achieve the desired performance.

Shape of the Blade Edge

Shaping the blade edge is a traditional technique used mostly on bench planes (jack, jointer, and smoothing) that greatly increases their effectiveness. The basic concept is this: the curvature equals the maximum thickness of the planed shaving. The strategy is effective for a number of reasons. On all planes, it keeps the corners of the blade from digging in and tearing up the wood at the borders of the cut. On roughing-out planes properly used diagonally to the grain, it reduces tearout, the amount of effort required to push the plane, and chip jamming at the most likely spot (the corners of the blade). On finish planes, it eliminates steps or ridges between each cut, producing a smoother surface. On jointer planes, the slight curvature can speed up jointing edges and strengthen the resulting edge joint.

But joinery planes should have a straight edge; the only possible exception to this I can think of is if you want to use a jack plane–sized rabbet plane for preparing timber as well as rabbeting. In this case I would have two sets of blades for the plane: one with the blade edge straight, the other with the edge prepared with the desired curve. Any plane used on a shooting board should also have a blade with a straight edge.

Length of Plane/Width of Blade

In the bench planes, long planes (14"–24" [350–600mm] and longer) true (straighten) surfaces. Their long length bridges low spots, with the blade cutting the high spots down and lowering all surface points to the same plane. Planes 12"–16" (300–400mm) long traditionally are used to prepare surfaces for the longer truing planes. Planes shorter than 12" (300mm) are used to smooth surfaces, with very short ones able to smooth the slightly less-than-flat surfaces by following the low spots rather than skipping over them as a longer plane would.

When making cabinets and furniture, most work will have been prepared with these planes before the joinery planes are used, so they only need to reference off these already prepared surfaces. More creative or exploratory work and some construction or restoration work, however, may not have this advantage, and the joinery plane may have to create its own reference surface. This may require making or modifying a plane to accomplish this. For instance, fitting dimensional lumber to irregular timber

Honing a Hollow-Ground Bevel

An argument against hollow grinding is that it thins the metal immediately behind the edge and produces a bevel angle that is too small. This happens because even though the edge is honed at the proper angle, the steel right behind that honed edge has been removed—hollowed out to the curve of the grinding wheel.

If you were to draw a tangent to the curve of the grind in the area immediately behind the honed edge, you would see this is a much smaller angle than the honing angle, and could allow the blade to flex.

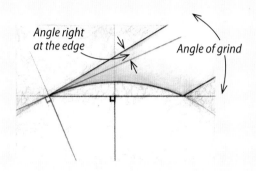

FIGURE 2-12. *The angle near the edge on a hollow-ground blade (shown here exaggerated for clarity) is much less than the overall angle to which the blade has been ground. On a ⅜" (9mm)–thick blade, such as a Japanese blade, ground to 30° on a 6" (152mm)–diameter wheel, the angle is roughly 7° less at the edge than the angle of grind, resulting in about a 23° edge angle—close to the minimum. With a 25° grind, the difference is even greater and results in an edge angle of less than 18°.*

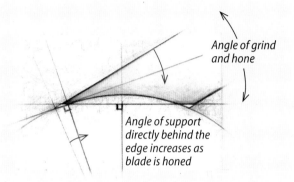

FIGURE 2-13. *As the blade is honed, the hollow decreases with each sharpening, and the angle directly behind the honed edge increases. Eventually, when the bevel has been honed flat, it equals the grind angle.*

such as log work can require long straight rabbets referenced independently from the irregular log surface. Traditional Chinese timber construction is also an example of such work: the natural curve of timbers is exploited for their strength and grace and even modified and exaggerated. Into these curved timbers partitions, panels, and screens are fitted into grooves and rabbets. The long rabbet plane was one of the carpenter's most valued tools for creating these joints. Modern studio furniture makers and artists explore uncommon shapes and combinations. The ability to create the joints to put these projects together will allow the woodworker to focus on creativity.

3

Plane Setup

Setup and tuning are similar for planes of all styles and functions, including planes for joinery. Basic procedures are performed in a specific order to set the plane up, followed by specifics for the type of plane you are preparing. These specifics will be handled in that tool's chapter.

• Inspect the plane for condition issues

• Prepare the blade

• Prepare the chipbreaker

• Bed the blade properly

• Configure the sole

• Adjust the mouth

Inspect the Plane

Metal

When checking out a plane, first look at the body. On all planes, the quality of the finish may give clues to what you can expect from the plane. Is it coarsely sanded or finely finished (even if it is nickel plated—or maybe because it's nickel plated!). What are the handles made of and how well are they finished? Inspect the body of a used plane carefully for cracks, especially around the bed and pressure points like the pivot pin on the level cap.

Most importantly, on all types of rabbet planes check *everything* for square: sides to sole, sides to blade bed, leading edge of the blade bed square to the length of the plane, a square blade edge that can be set parallel with the sole and be square to the length of the plane, and a mouth opening that is square and parallel both to the blade edge and the length of the plane. Fixing these issues on a wood plane can cause you a lot of work. If any are off on a metal plane (except perhaps an out-of-square blade edge), I would reject the plane.

On all models, check that the adjustment mechanisms will provide the settings you may require of the plane: heavy cut, very fine cut, fine mouth setting, etc. Sometimes the adjusters run out of adjustment at the extremes. Or when parts are moved, such as an adjustable throat, the parts go out of alignment.

Check the operation of the blade (depth) and lateral adjusters. See that they operate freely and are not distorted, bent, or broken, and engage the blade and chipbreaker fully.

If you get a real flea market find, you should take it totally apart and clean it, especially if there's any rust. This will also let you check more thoroughly for cracks and damage. Carefully unscrew all the screws; if they seem to be frozen, do not force them. Spray their base with some WD-40 or some similar release and let them soak until they can be loosened without danger of breaking. Clean dirt off with a brass or stainless steel brush; clean mating parts with red Scotch-Brite™ until they are totally clean. Brush screw threads off and put a drop of oil into their hole. You can clean and buff more, and even re-enamel, but you don't have to in order to get a functioning plane.

Old Wood Planes

On antique planes, inspect the body of the plane. Look for rot, or worse, and more commonly, beetle holes or wormholes. Avoid these. I once bought a transitional Bailey plane with a few beetle holes—the inside was nearly hollow. Beetle holes appear as tiny pinholes. However, do not mistake holes made from brads used to hold temporary fences nailed on by a previous owner for beetle holes. Holes from brads are acceptable, though sometimes hard to distinguish from beetle holes.

Often a body will shrink over time, especially if the plane was made on the

FIGURE 3-1. When I got this plane, luckily the wedge was already loose. Someone before me had trouble getting this wedge out; besides the splintering, notice the checked pattern near the top where someone locked on a pair of pliers to try and pull out the wedge. Needless to say, this wedge will have to be replaced.

East Coast or Europe and was moved to the West or Southwest; or was made in China or Southeast Asia and was imported to anywhere in the United States. The body will dry out and shrink around the blade, possibly causing the body to crack, or, at the very least, warp badly around the blade. If this is not too severe, the opening for the blade in the body can be carefully pared to give the blade more room (once you get the blade out). It may take quite a bit of work to get a frozen blade out, but don't get impatient and damage the body with a mallet trying to loosen the blade. Remember that on most of the old planes the blade is tapered, thicker at

the edge than the top, and is loosened by tapping it down: it will come out through the mouth. The wedge may stay behind and present more of a dilemma. Be patient here too, but you may end up having to remake the wedge, which is not that big of a deal. Damaging the body, however, is (**Figure 3-1**).

If the body is cracked at the bed, the plane may be useless, as this area is under a lot of stress, and re-gluing may not hold. Minor checks can often be tolerated; cracks around the throat, if not bad, can be injected with glue and clamped, or fitted with wood wedges that are then glued in. Handles can, of course, be refitted. Twists can be planed out, but if the distortion is too severe, squaring up the body and the blade bed to the flattened sole may remove too much wood at the wedge area on either side of the blade, weakening the plane and leaving it unstable.

Usually the mouth wears open on an old plane. If the plane is to be used for smoothing, a piece can be inlaid onto the bottom to close it up.

New Wood Planes

A new wood plane should require only tuning up of the sole rather than a major makeover.

With a new wood plane, it is always a good idea to pull the blade/chipbreaker assembly out and let the plane sit for a few months to allow it to acclimate to your shop. If your shop is drier than where the plane was made, this will save you the agony of trying to withdraw a blade seized by a shrunken body and the consequent possible damage to the plane. After the plane has acclimated, check the body for twist, and check that the blade has enough room on either side for lateral adjustment. If the plane body has twisted, then the blade bed may have some twist as well. Check the fit of the wedge to the body and chipbreaker, and check the mouth opening. Accept no checking or cracking (unless it is cracked around the blade because you failed to remove the blade). While checking or cracking might be tolerated on an old plane, there is no

need to have to deal with this on a new plane—it will only get worse.

After you have inspected your plane, either old or new, and have assessed the issues that have to be dealt with, you can begin to set up the plane.

Prepare the Blade

A new blade, or an old blade that needs to be rejuvenated, is always prepared by flattening the back first. If there are serious nicks in the blade, the bevel may be ground first to remove them, and then the back prepared. After the back has been flattened to a mirror polish, then the bevel is honed. Honing involves alternately stoning both the bevel and the back to remove the wire edge. Once the back has been polished, sharpening involves only touching up the back on the final polishing stone and not reworking it with all the stones used when first flattening it.

Ideally, the entire back should be flat (in a flat plane, the length and width of the usable edge steel). Practically, however, low spots can be allowed in this area as long as the area at the edge itself is at least 1/16" (2mm) wide and the full width of the blade. Low areas behind that will eventually get polished out as the blade is sharpened back with use. In the rare case this doesn't happen over time, the back can then be reflattened until the flat area at the blade edge is again continuous. Generally, with most joinery planes, since the blades are pretty narrow, flatness of the back is less critical than it might be for a bench or block plane style rabbet, or fillister plane, or any plane that also uses a chipbreaker.

Before starting, remove the chipbreaker, if there is one, and inspect the edge of the blade for damage. Then check the back for rust severe enough to cause pitting that is too deep to be honed out (**Figure 3-2**). Such pits, when the edge is sharpened down to them, will leave a track in the finish work. If the blade is to be used on a joint-forming plane, some minor pitting might be allowed, as either the joint won't show or it can be touched up with a joint–trimming plane. However, the blade will overheat in the area of these pits, rapidly dulling the blade and necessitating frequent re-sharpening or even regrinding.

After inspecting the blade, grind the bevel if necessary to remove any nicks and/or to shape the edge. Flatten the back down to a mirror polish, then go back and sharpen the edge (**Figure 3-3**).

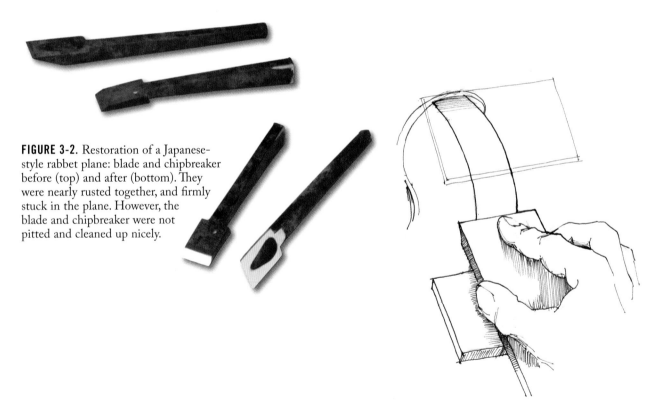

FIGURE 3-2. Restoration of a Japanese-style rabbet plane: blade and chipbreaker before (top) and after (bottom). They were nearly rusted together, and firmly stuck in the plane. However, the blade and chipbreaker were not pitted and cleaned up nicely.

FIGURE 3-3. Keeping a finger at the edge directly behind the bevel will tell you when the blade is becoming too hot. If the blade is too hot for your finger, it is too hot for the edge.

Flattening the Back of a Plane Blade

There are a number of techniques that can be used to flatten the back of a plane blade. Which technique is best is dependent upon how much work must be done to get it flat.

No matter which technique you use, you will have to finish with your sharpening stones. These must be flat, so start by flattening your sharpening stones. (See "Using and Maintaining Waterstones" on page 40.)

Before starting work on the blade, appraise the flatness of the back. Hold the blade up to a large light source, sighting along the blade so that you can catch a reflection that goes all the way across the back. Tilt the length of the blade up and down, and study the reflection. If the entire back lights up down to the edge, you have a dead flat blade, and you will only have to hone it through your usual series of stones. If only a portion of the length of the blade lights up and this light moves up and down the blade as you tilt it, then the blade has a curve to it; the shorter the reflection, the more the curve.

In this case, do not try to flatten the entire length of the blade. Only the lower portion—about ½" (13mm) minimum to about 1" (25mm) maximum—needs to be flattened, depending on your blade's curve. Flattening more is incredibly tedious, requiring the removal of a lot of steel. More importantly, it is not necessary to get a functioning blade.

Finally, look at the back edge itself. Tilt the blade until the reflection rolls down to the edge. If you have to tilt the blade more than a little to catch a reflection there, or if you can continue tilting the blade and continue getting a reflection, indicating a rounded edge, then a different strategy is called for. In this case, before starting to flatten the back, you should grind the main blade bevel back until the rounding or back bevel is eliminated.

After you have appraised the condition of the back of your blade, developed a strategy, and made sure your stones are flat, begin flattening by stroking the blade's back on your coarsest stone. Hold the blade perpendicular to the length of the stone, using the entire length of the stone and as much of the full width as possible, and stroke back and forth. Keep at least 1" (25mm) or more of the blade on the stone at all times.

Make sure the blade stays flat on the stone—no lifting or rocking. Keep pressure on the blade right behind the edge to keep from gouging the back. After about 30 seconds to a minute, clean and look at the back of the blade. If the new flat is within about ⅓₂" (0.8mm) of the edge at all places (check the reflection as before), you can probably continue using the waterstones for the whole process. Move to each individual stone as the polish pattern of each becomes continuous across and down to the entire edge.

If you have to spend more than about four or five minutes of continuous work on a waterstone, you will have to re-flatten it before continuing. Therefore, if a minute of vigorous work on the coarse stone leaves more than about ⅓₂" (0.8mm) of edge undone, you are probably better off going instead to a coarse diamond stone to flatten the blade. If not, you can wear your waterstones out of flat, necessitating re-flattening the stones (and most probably the back) several times before you are done. (If you have ceramic or Arkansas stones, you can probably do the whole flattening process on either of those. Just make sure they're flat before you start and remain flat as you work, as they do wear, albeit much more slowly.) After the flat on the back reaches the edge, you can go back and do your normal sharpening sequence on your (flat) stones to polish the back.

If after about a minute on your coarse stone you

Flattening the Back of a Plane Blade *(Continued)*

FIGURE 3-4. Add the carborundum and water to the center of the *kanaban* (iron plate). In the background is a stick that can be used when holding the blade.

show the new flat at ⅟₁₆" (2mm) or more away, consider measures that are more drastic (though you can continue to work away on the diamond stone if you prefer). The cheapest, fastest, and most effective way to flatten a badly out-of-flat plane-blade back is to use the Japanese method of carborundum (silicon carbide) on an iron plate (*kanaban*). The carborundum particles grip the softer *kanaban* (though it does wear it out—eventually), and abrades the tool steel. The iron flattening plate is available at Japanese tool suppliers, as well as carborundum, though if you can find a lapidary supply house you can get a lifetime supply very cheap.

The beauty of this method is the grit breaks down as you use it, so you can start with 60 or 90 grit, which is very coarse (for a blade in particularly bad condition), or 120 grit (if you think the blade is not too bad). Either gradually breaks down to about 6,000 grit, while increasingly refining the surface. In one step (and about 5 to 10 minutes of vigorous rubbing), you can go from a nasty old blade to a mirror-polished jewel.

To use the flattening plate, put about ¼ teaspoon of carborundum in the center of the plate and add 3 or 4 drops of water to it **(Figure 3-4)**. Begin rubbing the back of the blade back and forth using the whole length of the plate. Periodically bring the excess carborundum back into the center of the plate so all the carborundum is broken down at the same rate **(Figure 3-5)**. Stray coarse pieces of carborundum will

FIGURE 3-5. Rub the back of the blade back and forth using the whole length of the plate. Use of a stick allows you to increase the pressure on the blade at its edge while reducing finger fatigue. The blade and stick are held with the right hand, with the left hand keeping a constant downward pressure. Do not rock the blade. The blade must remain flat on the stone *at all times*. If you lift the right hand for even one stroke, you will round the edge enough to require 10 or 15 strokes to remove the damage.

FIGURE 3-6. The carborundum has broken down into a paste and is rubbed until dry.

scratch the blade, so make sure it is all used. Continue rubbing as the carborundum breaks down into a smooth paste, occasionally adding a drop or two of water if the paste gets too dry to rub. As the paste gets extremely fine, check your progress; you should see a consistent flat at the edge.

Continue rubbing until the back shows a high polish and the paste is transparently fine and rubbed dry (**Figure 3-6**). Then add 1 (or maybe 2) drops of water and vigorously rub until the paste is dry again. This will bring up a very high polish. Inspect the blade. Hopefully, the mirror polish of your newly flat back now extends all the way to the edge. If not, you will have to do it again, though you can probably start with 120 or 220 grit now. With the final polish, you do not have to follow up with any work on the stones; you can go right to the bevel.

Make sure to keep the carborundum separate from your stones, because it can embed itself and continue to scratch a blade for a long time. Wash the blade and everything else in separate water and rinse thoroughly.

Using and Maintaining Waterstones

Before use, synthetic waterstones need to be soaked for at least ten minutes, or until air bubbles stop coming out of the stone. If they do not have a wood base, you can store them indefinitely in water. A large, lidded plastic tub is good for this. If they have a wood base, you can still store them in water, but eventually the base will fall off. Synthetic finish stones (#3000 and above) generally do not need to be soaked, but check with the manufacturer and/or dealer.

Natural waterstones are never stored in water because doing so causes them to disintegrate. Coarser stones are soaked for 5 or 10 minutes before using and removed after sharpening. The natural finish stones generally do not need to be soaked, but again check with the seller. Natural stones will often crack if they are allowed to freeze, whether dry or in water.

The stones will have to be trued before they are used the first time as well as frequently trued as they are used. There are a number of ways to do this. My favored approach now is to use a diamond stone rubbed against the waterstone. I have been using the same diamond stone now for more than eight years and it has not worn out yet, so it is cost effective. Alternatively, you can use sandpaper—220-grit wet/dry on a piece of ¼" (6mm) plate glass laid on a flat surface.

However, you will get only about two flattenings before the sandpaper wears out, so costs can add up. In addition, sandpaper tends to glaze some stones (such as the Bester), so it is not always an option. I have also flattened stones on a concrete block, which works fine until the concrete becomes polished and the block wears out of flat. Also, a special stone is sold just for flattening sharpening stones, which works fine, but eventually it too gets glazed and out of flat.

FIGURE 3-7. Besides using a straight edge to check the stones for flat (which I find difficult when the stones are wet), you can check by using your flattening stone, which in this case is a diamond stone. A few strokes with the flattening stone will reveal the hollow, stained with the iron removed in sharpening.

FIGURE 3-8. Here the stone is almost restored to flat.

Some stones are harder than others, so the frequency of flattening will vary. Frequency also varies according to the task. A good procedure is to sharpen your straight-edge joinery blades first, right after flattening the stones. Then your smoothing planes and then bench planes of increasing blade curvature. That way you can actually use the wear of the stones to help shape the blade edges. You can even set aside old, badly worn stones to hone blades of significant curvature (like a scrub-plane blade).

In use, coarser stones are periodically washed clean and kept wet by adding a bit of water from the soaking container. The blade is abraded directly against the stone. The finish stones are kept barely wet, but not allowed to dry out; the slurry is allowed to build up, as this is what actually does the polishing, not direct contact with the stone. Using a *nagura* stone (a chalk stone available where water-stones are sold) raises the slurry more quickly.

FIGURE 3-9. Flat once again.

Prepare the Chipbreaker

Inspect the chipbreaker for a damaged or badly formed edge. If the problem is severe, see if you will have enough metal left after removing the damage to have a functioning chipbreaker; if not, replace it. Refine the shape of the top contour so there is a microbevel that meets the blade at an angle of about 50°, or such an angle that the combination of blade angle and chipbreaker angle totals 90° to 100°. If the particular configuration allows enough material to remain, put a large second bevel of about 25° behind the microbevel. (You will not be able to do this on a Stanley-type chipbreaker.) The second bevel improves chip clearance and helps eliminate throat clogging. Some of the after-market chipbreakers come with this configuration.

Next, hold the chipbreaker and the blade together in their final position, and then up to a light (**Figure 3-10**). No light should appear between the edge of the

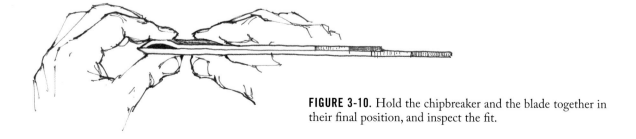

FIGURE 3-10. Hold the chipbreaker and the blade together in their final position, and inspect the fit.

chipbreaker and the back of the blade. Correct the edge of the chipbreaker if necessary, maintaining its geometry, by stoning the underside on a perfectly flat stone (**Figure 3-11**). If the edge is badly off, careful work with a smooth file may speed up this step, followed by careful stoning. Back-bevel the underside of the chipbreaker slightly so that it meets the blade at a knife's edge (**Figure 3-12**).

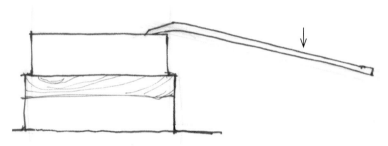

FIGURE 3-11. Position the chipbreaker on the stone slightly below horizontal to ensure the edge is slightly back-beveled.

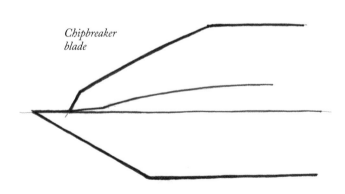

Chipbreaker blade

FIGURE 3-12. Undercut a degree or so to ensure contact at front edge.

Both the underside and the top microbevel closest to the edge should be stoned down to a polish (**Figure 3-13**). Finish the last strokes of the stoning on the top to ensure that the edge will meet tightly to the blade (**Figure 3-14**). Hold the chipbreaker and blade up to the light again (**Figure 3-10**) and check the fit. If the edge appears straight but is high on one corner and squeezing them together does not close the gap, twist the chipbreaker to straighten it. The edge should fully contact the blade and no light should show. Make sure that the chipbreaker is sprung slightly so that tightening its screw attachment brings the edge of the chipbreaker down tight to the blade (**Figure 3-15**). In some cases, the chipbreaker may have to be bent slightly to achieve this.

Attach the chipbreaker to the blade. Adjust its position according to the work to be done (setting the edge of the chipbreaker back a distance equal to the thickest shaving you're going to make with the plane). Check again that no light comes through the meeting of the two at the edge, and tighten the screw down.

Bed the Blade Properly

On all planes, double-check that the edge of the blade bed at the blade opening is square to the length of the plane (assuming the sole and sides are square to each other). If it isn't, then the blade bed is not square to the sides. You will have trouble making the blade parallel to the sole, and one side of the blade will want to cut deeper. This is basically not correctable on a metal plane. You can try to compensate for this by adjusting the blade. If the error exceeds the adjustment, though, then you will have to sharpen the blade out of square, parallel to the sole. This is a hassle that usually leads to a cascade of problems; it is not acceptable on a new plane. It also means that if you have an adjustable mouth, unless you file the mouth parallel to the blade, you will not be able to adjust the mouth down to a small opening and you will have trouble eliminating tearout. On wood planes, you can often pare the bed back into square.

Mouth Going out of Parallel

Taking too much off one side of the sole when flattening it can cause the mouth and back edge of the mouth opening at the frog to go out of parallel. The result is that both go out of square to the length of the plane. This is because the relief angle and blade-bed angle are acute angles and not square to the sole, resulting in their diverging rapidly as material is removed from the sole.

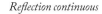
Reflection continuous

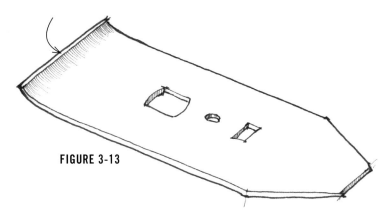

FIGURE 3-13

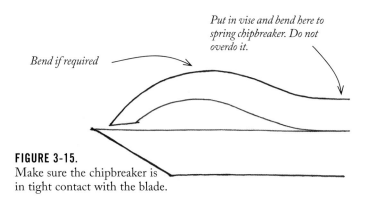

FIGURE 3-14.
Finish the last strokes stoning the chipbreaker on the top edge.

Stone

Top of chipbreaker

Put in vise and bend here to spring chipbreaker. Do not overdo it.

Bend if required

FIGURE 3-15.
Make sure the chipbreaker is in tight contact with the blade.

Bevel-Down Metal Planes

On a decent-quality metal plane, all of the surfaces of the blade seat and the back edge of the mouth opening will be nicely milled (check for square). At most, they will need only cleanup of a little bit of enamel or a recalcitrant corner or a bit of flash missed by the milling machine. Clean it up carefully with a file.

If you have a bevel-down bench plane style of rabbet such as a Stanley #10, remove the two screws residing under the blade that attach the frog to the body of the plane, and remove the frog. (Be certain the frog-adjustment screws do not protrude above the level of the bed when fully tightened and interfere with the bedding of the blade, as they might in some new versions of the plane.) Make sure the blade bed and the frog's mating surfaces are clean; a little bit of dirt under either one can cause the blade to chatter.

Inspect the frog and plane's mating surfaces for the same problems, and correct minor aberrations with a file

or diamond file as before. With the screws replaced but left slightly loose, see if it can be rocked on its mating surfaces. Experiment with the screws lightly tightened to verify the frog can be securely and solidly bedded. If it can't, this is very difficult to correct. Unless this is an otherwise particularly good plane or one of sentimental value, you should get another plane. If this is a new plane, definitely take it back. The mating surfaces are difficult to access with a file, particularly so when trying to keep things parallel and flat. Though I don't recommend it, if you want to try and correct it, you can use the "tapping" technique to discover the mating surface that is not making contact. Do this by holding down the frog tightly in the center with only one finger. Take a finger of the opposite hand and tap each of the four corners in turn. The corner that makes a tapping sound when struck is not making contact. Working on the frog and not the main body, take a little metal off the mating surface adjacent to it (on the same level) until the tapping sound stops. Hopefully, the frog remains workably square and parallel to everything when you're done, and you haven't made it worse.

Reinstall the frog and check that the opening of the mouth at the back (frog side) is square to the length of the plane, and that the frog can be made parallel to it.

Working around the Blade-Adjustment Nib

Because the blade-adjustment nib protrudes above the blade bed, is pinned, and cannot be removed, any overall flattening of the bed will have to be done piecemeal working around the nib. Working like this will most likely make its condition worse. Leave it alone. Just look for protrusions of enamel or missed milling. If the overall flatness of the bed is bad, get another plane.

The frog and the back of the throat at the body form the seat of the blade, and the two must be able to form a continuous flat plane (**Figures 3-16, 3-17, and 3-18**). Hopefully, the frog can be set back far enough and rotated if necessary to align with this edge.

Though a little bit of filing on the edge of the back of the mouth could be done if the frog cannot be rotated enough, I would recommend not doing this. It can bring about a cascade of problems, and blade adjustment will compensate (within limits) for out of square anyway.

Unless you are doing some exceptionally fine planing, adjust the frog to give the blade its maximum support, that is, aligned with the back edge of the mouth of the body. Insert the blade, making sure it is properly seated: the hole in the chipbreaker over the blade-adjuster nib, and the slot in the blade over the nib of the lateral-adjustment knob. Adjust the lever cap's screw so that there is only enough pressure to keep the blade from shifting around under its workload. Too much pressure creates a danger of damaging the plane.

Bevel-Up Metal Planes

While the separate bed, or frog, design of Stanley planes allows some small adjustability of limited usefulness, the bed on metal bevel-up planes is either done right or it isn't. It might have a small corner missed by the mill that you

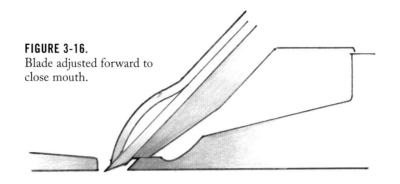

FIGURE 3-16.
Blade adjusted forward to close mouth.

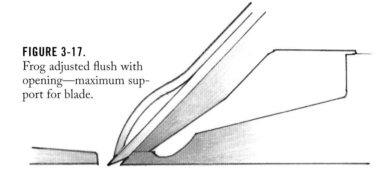

FIGURE 3-17.
Frog adjusted flush with opening—maximum support for blade.

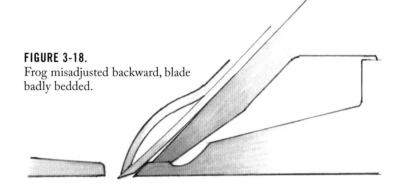

FIGURE 3-18.
Frog misadjusted backward, blade badly bedded.

might be able to file off, or on an old plane, a spot or two of compressed dirt raising the blade off the bed. Otherwise this is very difficult to correct. Usually any attempt to do so will make the situation worse.

Wood Planes

If your plane block has shrunk, you may first have to widen the escapement where the blade fits. You will also need a little additional room (± 1/32" [0.8mm]) to allow for lateral adjustment.

Check the blade seat for square by checking where the blade bed meets the sole: this edge should be square. Also, put the blade in and adjust it parallel to the sole making sure the edge of the blade is square. The blade edge should be square to the length of the plane, as well. Check for flat and lack of twist by sighting down the ramp or *blade bed*. Carefully pare this with a chisel

Marking

Because the surface of the blade bed on an old wood plane may be darkened with age and dirt, pencil lead may not read very well marking high spots for shaving. Try a China marker (wax pencil), crayon in red, blue, or white, machinist's bluing, or, surprisingly, Vaseline®, which will leave a glossy mark in contrast to the dull, darkened surface. Because the bearing area may be rather small, sometimes you may have to recoat and reinsert the blade several times to get a reading.

(or you can use a float if you have one) to take out the twist. Once you have the twist out, as best as can be visually determined, begin seating the blade. If the blade has a chipbreaker, screw it in its final position. If you have a tapered blade, check to see that its back (underside) is arched along its length. If it is, you will have to pay particular attention to the bed down near the sole and at the top of the plane, as that is where the blade will contact it. If your blade is parallel and not arched (some will arch with a chipbreaker attached), you will have to make sure the blade is contacting the bed at least at the bottom and top, similar to the tapered blade. Also ensure that it is not sitting on a high spot in between.

With both blades, you can check the flatness of the bed from top to bottom with a small straightedge and correct as necessary. After that, you can use the plane and see if the blade chatters. If not, you are all set. If it chatters in use, you can use the Japanese technique of rubbing pencil lead on the back of the blade and then rubbing the blade assembly in its position on its bed. Where the lead has rubbed off are the high spots. Ideally, you want to see substantial stains from the pencil over most of the length of the bed, especially down near the bottom (sole) of the plane. If you don't, pare away where the pencil has marked and repeat the process until the pencil marks the whole length of the bed and you get solid bearing across the bed at least at the bottom and the top.

Once you are confident the blade is well bedded, check the fit of the wedge: the wedge must fit well to both the blade and the plane body and be the correct taper. One way to check the fit is to tap down the wedge to working pressure and try to wiggle the blade and wedge at both the top and the bottom. If it wiggles at one and not the other, then the taper is incorrect. Take a light pass on the tight end of the wedge with a finely set plane and then straighten the cut the full length of the wedge so there is no belly on the edge. Try again until the wedge is tight at both ends and the blade holds its position.

Configure the Sole

The thinnest shaving a plane can cut is limited by the amount the sole or bottom of the plane is out of flat. If the sole is concave from end to end by ⅟₁₆" (2mm), for instance, the thinnest shaving you will be able to get from that plane will be about ⅟₁₆" (2mm). If you do manage to get it to cut (usually when half the plane is off the board), eventually the board will become convex, curved to match that of the sole of the plane. The clue that a plane bottom is not flat is that the plane goes from not cutting at all to cutting too deeply without any ability to cut any shaving in between. The rabbet planes are particularly susceptible to pressure from the blade clamping mechanism distorting the bottom and holding the blade off the work. This is because there is no way to support the blade all the

way to its edge and still be able to cut into corners to make a rabbet. The blade bed cantilevers out unsupported and flexes under the pressure. This is where you must focus your attention when flattening the sole of a rabbet, fillister, shoulder, bullnose, and dado plane.

The tricky part is not destroying square. On all planes, you want to remove only enough material to bring this area under the blade in line with the rest of the sole.

A wood plane bottom flattens differently than a metal plane bottom. First, it is never sanded. I know this goes counter to most of what you will read, but there are good reasons for it. Sanding embeds grit into the bottom of the plane which is released gradually during use of the plane. (For the same reason, you should never plane a surface that has been previously sanded, as the grit left in the surface will also rapidly dull a plane blade.) Anyway, sanding is too slow and tedious if any amount has to be taken off, and too indefinite in its results.

With the blade wedged down to working pressure (this is important!), but retracted from the bottom about ⅟₁₆" (2mm), put a straightedge across the area immediately in front of the mouth and check to see if this is straight. Check the body for twist with winding sticks, and then check along its length.

If the plane must be corrected ⅟₁₆" (2mm) or more, then you may want to run it over the power jointer, or plane it carefully with another plane (**Figure**

3-19). When running a plane over the power jointer, always remove the blade assembly! There is too much danger that the blade will loosen under the vibration of the cut or more material will be removed than anticipated, and the blade will contact the power jointer's cutters, an extremely dangerous occurrence. After the work with the power jointer, the blade assembly can be reinstalled

Gauging Straightness

You can use feeler gauges under a straightedge to measure the amount a surface is out of flat, but it is easier to gauge the amount just by sighting under a straightedge: the human eye can see light through a gap of less than 1/1000" (0.025mm).

FIGURE 3-19. Preparing the sole of a wood rabbet plane. Besides the split that had to be repaired, this plane had a broken nail embedded in its sole that had to be set below the surface before it could be planed.

to finish preparing the bottom. With either the power jointer or another plane, remove as little material as possible. The first cut with either should remove just a whisper of a shaving. Better to remove too little than misjudge and remove too much. The best technique will be a series of light passes, each cut being as productive and removing as little material as possible. Check for square after each cut.

Put the blade back in the plane, and then adjust it so it is withdrawn from the sole a good 1/32" (0.8mm) under working pressure. Hold a straightedge on the bottom of the plane and up to the light. Most probably the area immediately under the blade will protrude and not be in line with the sole in front of the blade. Use another lightly set plane to remove this area and flatten the sole. Put the joinery plane in a vise upside down, and put the working plane on the sole of the joinery plane so that its blade is at the blade opening of the joinery plane. Keeping pressure on both planes at the area before the blade of the joinery plane, take a shaving off the area of the sole behind the blade of the joinery plane. You should be cutting a shaving only in the area after the blade. Keep the cutting plane referenced on the joinery plane sole in front of the blade: usually the plane will stop cutting before it reaches the end of the joinery plane (you don't want to follow the bottom). You should only have to do this once or twice to bring the sole into line **(Figure 3-20)**.

With a metal plane, I have found a lot of sanding results in a distorted bottom rather than a flat one. I think the distortion results from the slight repetitive error in weight shift that happens over lots of strokes. If you have had some experience in sharpening, you know you can take more material off one part of the blade simply by putting more pressure on that area. This is especially a concern with all types of rabbet planes as the sides must remain square to the sole, as well as the sole flat and straight. You must work with concentration, purposefully rubbing each stroke and not mindlessly scrubbing. Check the bottom and check for square every three or four strokes. Note the pattern of the sandpaper on the sole: is it more on one side or another? It should be about the same. Has the sanding pattern extended to include the mouth area? If it has, then you are done. Note that you can put more pressure on the back of the plane or front and really slow your progress removing material under the bed of the plane. You want to focus your attention right at the blade edge so that the area under the blade ends up being on the same plane as the area in front of the plane.

Check the Sole

It is important to have the blade assembly installed, under full working pressure, as the pressure from the lever cap distorts the sole and this must be corrected during this process. Retract the blade about 1/16" (2mm) from the bottom

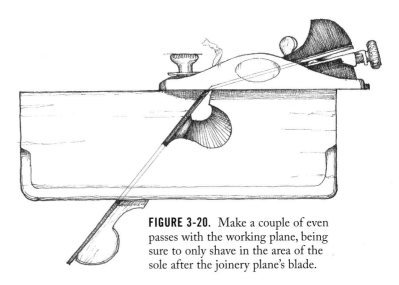

FIGURE 3-20. Make a couple of even passes with the working plane, being sure to only shave in the area of the sole after the joinery plane's blade.

to avoid contacting the blade edge when working. Using a good straightedge against the bottom, hold the two up to the light to check for high spots. Check all across the bottom, especially the area right in front of the mouth, as well as diagonally and perpendicular to the length. Check for twist with winding sticks.

You can use wet/dry sandpaper, micron-graded plastic-backed abrasives, or adhesive-backed sandpaper. Tape (or adhere) one or two pieces (depending on the length of the plane and the size of abrasive sheet you are using) to a flat surface such as a jointer bed. A granite platen is best but not necessary. Make sure your surface is flat. Just because it is a milled surface, such as a table saw, does not mean it is flat. (My table saw is not, unfortunately.)

If you do not have a machined surface you can or want to use, a flat worktop will do. Put a piece of 1/4" (6mm) float glass over it to bridge any minor surface irregularities. (If the surface underneath the glass is not flat, the glass will flex under pressure.) You can even use MDF if it is well supported and you're not using water. Using water with wet/dry sandpaper will keep the paper from clogging and holds the sandpaper in place on a sheet of plate glass. Wet or dry, but especially wet, sanding will make a mess, so protect the surface you are working on. I think 180 grit is a good compromise between fast cutting and sufficient polishing. You can always use a fine metal polish or even toothpaste afterward to polish the surface without distorting the bottom.

Do not do this metal work on your bench! The metal filings will infect your workpieces for years to come, not only dulling tools but showing up in the work, sometimes years later, as black dots or splotches, as the filings slowly rust.

Adjust the Mouth

Having finished the bottom, inspect the mouth. The mouth should be straight, sharp where it meets the sole, and crisply formed. Insert the blade assembly and adjust the blade to a working position, making sure the blade edge is parallel to the sole (and the blade edge is square). The mouth opening should also be parallel to the blade edge.

Most old wood planes will have the mouth worn quite open. This is not much of a problem for joint-forming planes. But if you want to use your plane for joint-trimming and want to reduce tearout, there are two things you can do. You can shim the blade: this will move the blade forward and reduce the mouth opening. I usually use paper for this, but would not use any more than three layers of bond paper. If this doesn't close the mouth sufficiently, then you will have to take more drastic measures and cut the sole off and replace it. See page 74 for more info on restoring a rabbet plane.

On a metal plane, all you can do is shim the blade, but I wouldn't put more than two layers of paper under it.

PART 2:
The Planes

4

Rabbet Planes

The term "rabbet plane" is often used as an umbrella term covering a variety of planes with slightly different functions. By definition, a rabbet plane is a plane whose blade projects to the edge of the sole on one or both sides of the plane. This allows it to cut right into the corner of a stepped cut—called a rabbet (also, a rebate)—something a bench plane cannot do. Technically, a rabbet plane doesn't have a fence: a rabbet plane with a fixed fence is called a fillister plane. A rabbet plane with a movable fence is called a moving fillister plane, though often in day-to-day, use the distinction between any of them will be ignored. While a rabbet plane can be used to form a rabbet, its primary use now is usually to fine-tune it. Rabbet planes with fences are primarily joint-forming planes usually used to make the joint. And most of these planes come in two versions: one with the blade square to the cut, and the other with the blade skewed to the cut.

FIGURE 4-1. The classic rabbet plane has been largely unchanged for centuries. The form of this plane can be found in nearly all woodworking cultures.

FIGURE 4-2. A typical Japanese shouldered-blade rabbet plane.

The Basic Rabbet Plane

The basic rabbet plane's most common (and possibly earliest) form has a narrow blade captured in a relatively tall and narrow block of wood. The height gives greater control, a good grip, and greater depth of cut (**Figure 4-1**). This form, with only slight variation, is found not only throughout Europe and America, but also in China and Japan—even though their bench planes look very different from Western forms. The blade is bedded with the bevel down (usually), at any of the angles you might find in the bench planes—from 40° to 70° and above—though 45° to 60° are the most common angles to be found now. It may or may not have a chipbreaker. The blade may be mounted square to the length of the plane, or it can occasionally be found with a skewed blade, the mouth open on one or both sides. This skewing of the blade is done to ease making cross grain rabbets (and possibly the occasional dado after the shoulders of the dado are saw cut). Also, the planes can occasionally be found with a cross grain cutting "spur," or cutter. This is used to score the grain and keep the shoulder of the cut from tearing up when used across the grain. If the plane has spurs on both sides of the plane, then it is technically a dado plane (see Chapter 6 on page 91).

Taking the blade to the full width of the sole is done in different ways. The most common nowadays is to have a T-shaped or spade-shaped blade—called a shouldered blade. The blade is wide at the sole and narrows above to pass through and be captured by the body of the plane (**Figure 4-3**). This style is used in both wood- and iron-body planes. Alternatively, the blade can be full width for its entire length, with the body flaring on one or both sides of the plane a distance above the sole of the plane. This is common on older wood-body planes as well as contemporary German wood-body planes and many iron-body planes as well. This may limit the depth of the cut on deep rabbets, as the body eventually gets in the way. But, while this might be an issue in timber framing and carpentry, for the vast majority of cabinet and furniture work it is not a problem.

The size of this style of rabbet plane varies widely, from less than 6" (152mm) long to more than 12" (300mm). The

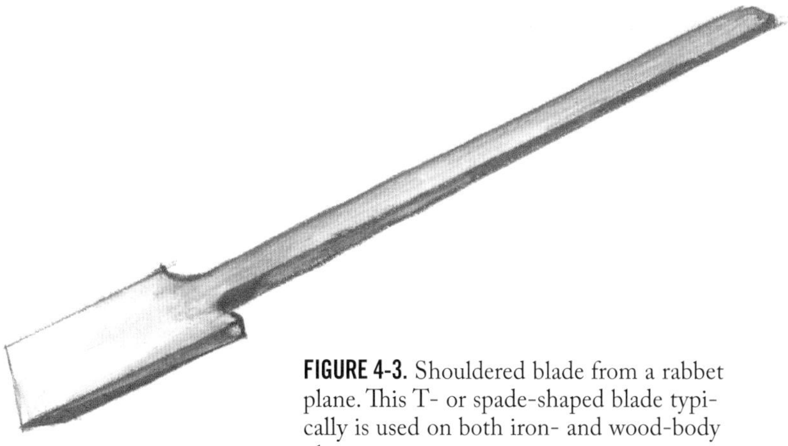

FIGURE 4-3. Shouldered blade from a rabbet plane. This T- or spade-shaped blade typically is used on both iron- and wood-body planes.

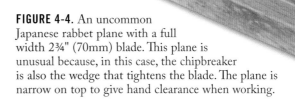

FIGURE 4-4. An uncommon Japanese rabbet plane with a full width 2¾" (70mm) blade. This plane is unusual because, in this case, the chipbreaker is also the wedge that tightens the blade. The plane is narrow on top to give hand clearance when working.

Chinese will often use a rabbet plane 16"+ (400mm+) long and from about ½" (13mm) or as little as ¼" (6mm) wide, to maybe 1½" (38mm).

Rabbet planes wider than this tend to be variations of bench planes with blades up to 2¼" (57mm), though I do have a Japanese rabbet plane that is 2¾" (70mm) wide, an exceptional width.

Rabbet Bench and Block Planes

There are also rabbet planes that are bench planes in form but redesigned to cut rabbets by having the sides of the plane body cut open and using a T-shaped blade to extend fully to the sides. An example of this is the Stanley #10, originally called a Carriage Maker's Rabbet Plane. First introduced in 1870, it is a jack plane–sized plane that has had its sides cut away to accommodate a full width blade. This plane is 13"–14" (330–355mm) long with a blade 2⅛" (54mm) wide. There was also a #10¼ version with cross grain cutting spurs and tilting handles to keep your hands from getting banged on the sides of deep rabbets. There is also a #10½ version that is 9" (228mm) long and has an adjustable mouth.

Currently, Lie-Nielsen is producing their version of the #10¼, using the Bedrock format that allows relatively easy adjustment of the mouth opening by adjusting the frog, something more difficult to do on the original (**Figure 4-5**).

Both Lie-Nielsen and Lee Valley are producing their own low-angle (blade bevel mounted up) version of the jack rabbet. Lie-Nielsen's version is 12¾" (324mm) long and 2" (50mm) wide with a 12° bedding angle and Lee Valley's version is 15⅛" (384mm) long and 2¼" (57mm) wide with a 15° bedding angle. Both of these have cutting spurs on both sides. Since they have bevel-up blades, they have the ability to vary the cutting angle by changing the bevel angle of the edge of the blade and thus improve the quality of the cut on difficult woods. The Lee Valley jack rabbet has an independently adjustable mouth, a tilting rear handle, and the ability to attach a fence, but costs about 30% more than the Lie-Nielsen (**Figure 4-6**).

Also available are rabbet block planes. Lie-Nielsen has a version with

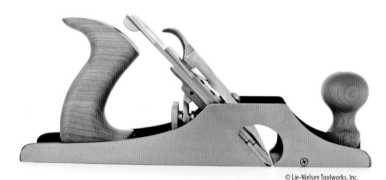

© Lie-Nielsen Toolworks, Inc.

FIGURE 4-5. Lie-Nielsen's new, improved version of Stanley's #10¼ Carriage Maker's Rabbet Plane, complete with nickers, tilting handles, and a Bedrock-style frog.

© Lee Valley Tools Ltd.

FIGURE 4-6. Veritas's bevel-up jack rabbet plane with tilting handle, fence, and adjustable cutting spurs.

the blade edge at 90° to the length of the plane, and a skewed-blade version both right and left with a fence. Neither style of plane, however, has an adjustable mouth.

Skewed-Blade Rabbet Planes

A useful form of rabbet plane (possibly the most useful) is the skewed-blade rabbet plane. Here the edge of the blade is angled about 15°–22° and up to 30° to the length of the plane, the lead point of the blade projecting fully to one side of the plane. This angling of the blade tends to pull the plane into the shoulder of the work, making good registration on the work easier. It is also very useful for cross grain planing, something which happens surprisingly frequently, such as sizing tenons. They are also useful for fielding or smoothing panel edges, both with and across the grain.

The traditional wood form of the rabbet plane can sometimes be found with a skewed blade (**Figure 4-7**).

The Japanese also make an excellent version of the skewed-blade rabbet plane, often with a top-quality blade and chipbreaker. While I realize that this may require a shift in habits and skill sets, I can highly recommend them and encourage woodworkers to explore these planes. (For more information, see my book *Discovering Japanese Handplanes*.) The use of a chipbreaker in these planes increases the quality of the cut and the planes' versatility.

Lee Valley also makes a skewed-blade rabbet in an iron block plane, both

FIGURE 4-7. In the foreground are a right- and left-hand skew-blade Japanese rabbet planes. These planes are open only on their respective sides; that is, the blades do not cut the full width of the sole. In the background, a typical Western-style skew-blade rabbet plane with a full-width blade, open on both sides.

© Lee Valley Tools Ltd.

FIGURE 4-8. Veritas's skewed-blade rabbet block plane.

right and left, with a fence and adjustable mouth, increasing the versatility of the plane (**Figure 4-8**). And Lie-Nielsen is making a new, improved version of the old Stanley 140 skewed-blade block plane in bronze. The original Stanley had an inherent weakness in that the blade was only supported by one rather thin side of the plane body. This resulted in some flex when the side plate was removed for rabbeting work. Lie-Nielsen has improved this by doing a thicker section and making the plane more rigid, but it still seems like a patch on a nice but flawed Stanley design. Plus you've got another part to deal with in attaching and detaching the side.

The Stanley Rabbet Planes

Stanley made a series of what they called Cabinetmaker's Rabbet Planes, though with their proportions and low-angle bevel-up blade, they more closely resemble shoulder planes. There is the #90—which is a bullnose plane—and the #92, #93, and #94, similar in design, but varying in length, from 4" (102mm) for the #90, and 5½" (140mm), 6½" (165mm), and 7½" (190mm) respectively for the #92, #93, and #94. Design-wise, these would seem to be ideal: a versatile size, relatively comfortable in the hand, with an adjustable mouth and the ability to be taken apart and made into either a chisel plane (#92, #93, #94) or a bullnose/chisel plane (#90). They also have a low blade angle, making them usable for trimming the end grain of shoulders as you would use a shoulder plane. They have an adjustable mouth that allows the mouth to be closed down to reduce the tearout that you might get with such a low cutting angle. But sadly I've never seen one that was machined well enough to be of much use; the parts are often badly out of line. However, Stanley has begun making a revised version of the #92 in their Sweet Heart line. This is by all reports a decent plane, far exceeding its predecessors in quality (**Figure 4-9**).

The Stanley 90 series of rabbet planes begins to approach the proportions of a shoulder plane, alternately being referred to as both rabbet planes and shoulder planes in the literature. In this same style and size of plane is the Record #311, often called the 3-in-1 plane, now made by Clifton and numbered 3110. It is, as its name says, three planes in one: rabbet plane, bullnose plane, and chisel plane (and because of its low blade angle, a shoulder plane). These are good (and expensive) planes worth your consideration, despite the price. (There is more on bullnose and chisel planes starting on page 100.) Many

FIGURE 4-9. Stanley's new #92 shoulder and chisel plane.

© Stanley Black & Decker, Inc.

FIGURE 4-10. The Clifton 3-in-1 plane disassembled: chisel plane, bullnose piece, and rabbet-plane nosepiece.

Record planes from this period were of dubious quality, but the 3-in-1 was well made. However, in my model (now about 40 years old—the lowest point of Record's quality in their other planes), there is no method for adjusting the mouth. While it is relatively narrow (about 1/32" [0.8mm]), it is still too big to control difficult tearout. The new Clifton planes come with a couple of shims to open the mouth up, so this implies that the plane comes with a tight mouth. I have not been able to examine these new planes to verify that. I do find bullnose and chisel planes less useful than I would have thought, though sometimes nothing else works (**Figure 4-10**).

Which One?

Here's what you need to consider:

- If you are fine-tuning a cut rabbet, whether cut by machine or by hand, you have to have the ability to make a smooth cut, one that avoids tearing out the grain. This means you must have at least one of the tactics available for reducing tearout: either a chipbreaker, the ability to achieve a small mouth opening, or possibly an appropriate cutting angle. Preferably, you'll have all three.

- The size of the rabbets you are tuning will determine the size of the plane.

- If you are smoothing cross grain cuts, you will have to have a skewed blade.

If you have more time than money, you might want to set up a used traditional wood rabbet plane. Even if it doesn't have a chipbreaker, a new sole can be fitted (this often has to be done anyway) to give a fine mouth opening. This will reduce the use of this plane to only making fine shavings, however.

The modern versions of the traditional wood rabbet plane, such as ECE and Primus, can be found with adjustable mouths and chipbreakers. The light weight and low friction of wood on wood, combined with the precision Primus adjuster, is an attractive combination. H.N.T. Gordon makes an excellent rabbet plane in this style with a blade bedded at 60° for use in tropical hardwood. If you turn the blade around, the cutting angle becomes 90°, making it an excellent rabbet-scraper for woods that just will not be planed.

If you can find a well-machined Stanley #92, #93, or #94 rabbet plane, I could recommend that as a first plane. I have yet to find a well-machined one. The Clifton 3110, which was my first rabbet plane (well, actually, it was a Record 311) is another option, but it was expensive when I bought it, and still is. If, however, you think or know you will eventually need a chisel and bullnose plane, this could end up saving you money.

Personally, I use a rabbet plane largely for joint trimming and smoothing machine-made rabbets. I may use a moving-fillister plane for forming the joint when machine setup is awkward or dangerous, or when I just feel it's going to be faster than setting up a machine. Though a fillister plane can also be used for trimming, the fence is often in the way, requiring adjustment or removal.

Since I am primarily making precise trimming cuts on the rabbets, which requires good control, I like a wider plane that sits lower. I can be down and balanced on the work, usually using a Japanese skewed-blade plane or the skewed-blade block plane, such as the Lee Valley, for work on tenons, for instance. At around 1½" (38mm) wide, I find this size of rabbet plane to be more useful, as it does not make any difference how much the plane hangs out beyond the rabbet. These planes are not so wide or long as to cause balance problems on shorter pieces.

I also prefer the skewed-blade rabbet planes because I think they are more versatile, though you may eventually have to buy two planes, a right and left. A rabbet plane is often used across the grain—to pare the thickness of a tenon or a tongue, for instance. A skewed blade works at an angle to the grain, rather than perpendicular to it, resulting in a much smoother cut. It also can be used to form or smooth the field on a door panel (two of the four fielding cuts on a panel are cross grain), a cut that will show and must be smooth. A blade cutting directly perpendicular to the grain will only tear the surface. The skewed blade also can hog off more wood with or across the grain, with less resistance, than a blade bedded perpendicular. The drawback is that these planes rarely come with cutters wider than around 1½" (38mm). If you consistently do

larger work, then accuracy in trimming is strained by having to make repeated overlapping passes. If you find yourself doing consistently larger work, you may have to invest in one of the jack rabbet planes and just expect to sand a lot where cross grain work shows.

Another difficulty with skewed-blade rabbet planes can be encountered if you work with tropical hardwoods. The effectiveness of a skewed blade is lost on these woods when cutting with the grain, though it still cuts superbly across the grain. To get good results with the grain in tropical hardwoods, you may have to use a rabbet plane with a cutting angle around 60°, the cutting edge perpendicular, not skewed. (For setting up and tuning the rabbet plane, see page 65.)

Now, having just said that I prefer a low, wide profile with a skewed blade for trimming rabbets and tenons, I'm going to backtrack a bit. For rabbets up to about ¾" (19mm), I find myself reaching for my shoulder plane more and more. I don't use it on tenon faces because it is too narrow and less accurate (and you can use a paring chisel or a router plane to do that as well). On narrow rabbets along the edges of boards, I find the high profile makes it easier to gauge whether I am at 90° to the work. And the new high-quality planes are well made with an easily adjustable mouth that allows me to control the cut, so I am able to both hog off heavy shavings and make fine, smooth cuts.

But for overall versatility, I would have to choose the Japanese or iron skewed-blade block plane. It is possible to trim a tenon shoulder with a rabbet plane, but it is less satisfactory to trim wide rabbets, such as tenons with a shoulder plane.

Using the Rabbet Plane

While the basic unfenced rabbet plane is now used mainly for tuning up already-cut rabbets, it certainly can be used to form rabbets, or even V cuts. You will need to clamp a straightedge to the work at the cut line if the rabbet is parallel to the grain. If the rabbet is perpendicular to the grain, you will have to also use a knife to score the fibers along the straightedge before you begin (unless the plane has a "nicker," or scoring blade), and usually score again several times as the work progresses. Without a clean knife cut, the blade will tear and not cut the end grain fibers of the shoulder of the rabbet, leaving a rough surface.

When cutting a rabbet square to the face of the piece, continuous attention must be paid to the position of the plane maintaining 90°. After a few strokes, and periodically after that, check the work with a square, both for the bottom being parallel to the face, and that the side of the rabbet has not "stepped out," an issue with the blade setting.

You can also form a with-the-grain rabbet or even a V cut without a fence using just the plane itself to establish the edge of the cut. Tilt the plane 45° on its corner and, short of the final marked line, cut an initial V groove (you can't do this with a skewed-blade rabbet plane, unfortunately). When establishing the cut, it is often easiest to begin just a few inches from the far end of the board (if you are using a push plane), and extend the cut a few inches on each pass, rather than trying to establish the cut for the entire length in one pass. (If you are using a pull plane, you will have to begin the cut nearest to you, and extend the cut away from you on each pass.) This works for both the V cut and the rabbeting cut. As the V cut gets deeper, you may need to flip the plane occasionally to plane the other face of the groove. If you are making a rabbeting cut, this is the initial reference shoulder of the rabbet. Then, referencing the plane against this shoulder, make repeated passes, rotating the plane a few degrees on each pass until you reach your depth and the angle you want for the bottom of the rabbet (best to mark this on the edge of the board). Once you reach that depth, you can turn the plane on its side and finish planning the vertical shoulder of the rabbet back to the marked line. This technique is a virtual necessity if your rabbet has a compound taper or if this joint is made more complicated by the two faces being greater than 90°. If they are less than 90°, the faces of the rabbet will have to be finished to the required angle using a side-rabbet plane (see Chapter 10 on page 116).

Cutting a Rabbet Freehand

1   To cut a rabbet freehand, begin by marking the cut lines all around the rabbet. Then, starting at the far end of the board, make a short cut with the edge of the plane, well away from the shoulder line.

2   Tilt the plane to make a V groove. (Note: You can't do this with a skewed-blade rabbet plane.)

3   Extend the cut 2" (50mm) or 3" (76mm) at a time, progressing back toward you. Always keep the front edge of the plane in the already-made portion of the groove as you begin the next cut. This will help keep the plane from skipping around.

4 The V groove is not sharply tilted, the plane leaning about 15°.

5 With the V groove fully established for the length of the rabbet, you can begin to make square cuts to bottom out the rabbet.

6 The rabbet flat, parallel and to the cut line. Now you can clean up the shoulder.

Cutting a Rabbet Freehand *(Continued)*

7 Laying the plane flat on the rabbet, cut squarely back to the shoulder.

8 The completed rabbet.

Setting Up Rabbet Planes

The same procedures, in the same order, are followed when setting up the rabbet plane as described in Chapter 3: Plane Setup (see page 32). Additionally, some things are specific to the plane, as follows.

1. Inspect the Plane

The most important thing to know about a rabbet plane is that the blade must be able to protrude on its cutting side(s) about 1/64" (0.4mm) or maybe a little less. This seems counterintuitive, but is proven with experience: unless the blade protrudes slightly, the plane will step away from the cut line as the cut deepens, resulting in an out-of-square shoulder and a generally narrower rabbet. I think this happens because when wood is cut there is a slight bit of compression and then springback. Though this is virtually negligible on a single cut, with repeated cuts it's additive. This is particularly true because the side of the blade is not actually cutting the fibers, but tearing them away.

Check, when you first get the plane, that the blade is slightly wider than the plane body. (The check is not necessary on a one-sided rabbet plane, obviously. Just make sure the blade can be positioned proud of the side.)

If for some reason the blade exceeds 1/64" (0.4mm) on both cutting sides (unlikely on a metal plane, but an old wood-body plane can have shrunk or been worn away by at least that much), then the blade can be carefully ground narrower. If the blade is too narrow on a metal-body plane, you will have to get a new blade—or a new plane. While the blade can sometimes be pushed to the working side to accommodate a too-narrow blade, there is no reason to have to deal with it on a new plane. And if the blade cannot be pushed to the side, tilting the blade toward that side is not a satisfactory solution. Both the blade and the plane are ground square, and tilting the blade puts the edge out of parallel with the sole. On a wood-body plane, the body can be planed down to achieve the required protrusion.

Site along the sole or use a straightedge. Oftentimes the front and back portions of the sole will have twisted out of line; this is especially true of an old plane. On a new plane, there should be little of this: if the sole is straightened, you will be removing material usually in the area of the blade, thus reducing the plane's width. The blade will then protrude too far, necessitating grinding the blade. I would consider returning such a new plane. On an old plane, this is quite common, almost to be expected. This area can be sawn off if bad enough and replaced, or the blade lightly ground narrower. Theoretically, you paid less for this plane.

The Correct Blade Projection on a Rabbet Plane

Setting the edge of the blade of a fillister or any form of rabbet plane dead flush to the side of the plane will most probably result in the cut drifting away from the shoulder line as repeated cuts are made.

While in theory setting the blade of a rabbet or shoulder plane flush to its side would seem the logical thing to do, in practice the blade should be set slightly proud of the side, otherwise the cut will tend to "step out" at each stroke. You won't notice this until you've cut down a bit. It seems illogical that this would work, but I think it's because wood always compresses a bit when cut and has a little spring-back. This makes all the more sense when you realize that the side of the cut is actually being torn away by the side of the blade and not sheared with a cutting edge. Even with a nicker, especially on end grain, there tends to be a bit of compression and springback. This bit of springback tends to push the plane out from the shoulder cut on the next pass, causing it to step out. You effectively have to overcut at the shoulder the amount of the springback to keep the cut straight.

How much should the blade project? Only as much as it takes to stop the stepping and not tear up the wood beyond the shoulder line. Tage Frid, at one point, recommended ¹⁄₆₄" (0.4mm) projection. That seems a bit strong, but I've had it work. More likely, if your blade is sharp, only a few thousandths of an inch will suffice. Surprisingly, I've found that a very slight projection beyond the scoring blade can be helpful as well; this is probably because either the point or edge of the blade, or the spur, or both, are not sharp enough. But if it's tearing up beyond the score line, then it's set too deep. Keep an eye on it or do a test piece.

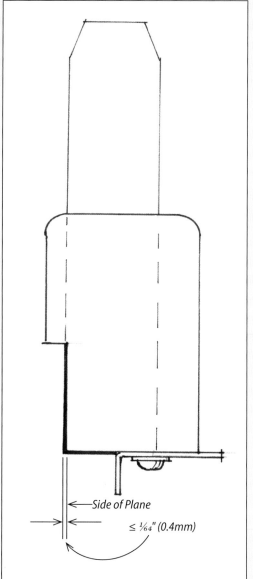

Side of Plane

≤ ¹⁄₆₄" (0.4mm)

FIGURE 4-11. All types of rabbet planes, including the fillister, should have the blade adjusted to project slightly beyond the side of the plane when in use.

2. Prepare the Blade

After inspecting your plane—and establishing that you have the correct width blade—begin setting it up by sharpening the blade. As described in the general procedure "Prepare the Blade" on page 35, flatten the back first. The bevel must then be sharpened straight across, with no curvature. It must be square enough to its length so it can be made parallel to the sole within the plane's range of adjustment (usually not very much). With a skewed-blade rabbet plane, you will have to establish (or maintain) the correct angle of the blade to accomplish the same parallel relation to the sole. You will not be able to check it with a square, so, if you have lost the correct angle, it may take some putting it in and out of the plane to get it right. I suggest that if you buy a new skewed-blade plane, you immediately make an accurate template of the blade for future reference should you later have to grind the blade.

The sides of the blade must be sharp, especially where it comes right down to the corners. All rabbet planes have some back beveling on the sides of the blade. Sometimes there will be a narrow area that is 90° or less to the face of the blade, but this should be sharp. Many blades, and all skewed blades, have a significant back bevel that comes straight down to a sharpened edge where it meets the skew point. These sharp beveled edges are

FIGURE 4-12. Besides the split that had to be repaired, this plane had a broken nail embedded in its sole that had to be set below the surface before it could be planed true. The split is opened up with a thin kerf saw, and then a tapered sliver is tapped in and glued, and then trimmed flush when the glue is dry.

relieved to not only clear the work but also provide a cleaner cut to the shoulder of the rabbet.

3. Prepare and Fit the Chipbreaker

If there is a chipbreaker, fitting it is pretty much the same as with a bench plane. You can refer to the general procedures "Prepare the Chipbreaker" on page 41.

4. Bed the Blade Properly

Inspect the blade bed for flaws. I strongly suggest you do not touch this area on a metal plane, because it is difficult to access and easy to mess up. If you have a flaw, return the plane and get another. The bed on a wood plane is prepared as described in the general setup section.

5. Configure the Sole

It is only with great reluctance that I attempt to condition the sole of a metal rabbet plane, because it is too easy to lose square between the sides and the sole in trying to flatten either. If the sides are not square to the sole, I suggest you return the plane; I think it is just too difficult to correct for squareness on a metal rabbet plane, and you shouldn't have to on a new one, anyway. However, the basic design of most rabbet (and especially shoulder) planes leaves the bed under the blade pretty thin with little mass to support the blade where the pressure is greatest. Sometimes you might find that when trying to get a thin, clean shaving to smooth a rabbet that the plane will not cut when adjusted for a fine cut. This is because the lever cap has pushed the bed of the plane slightly out of alignment with the rest of the sole of the plane, preventing the blade from cutting. If backing off the pressure on the lever cap does not remedy the situation (you should only have enough pressure to keep the blade from shifting—and that is often not very much), then some flattening of the sole will have to be done. This should be as minimal as possible, just enough to remove a bit of the sole under the blade to bring the sole into line when the plane is used.

Tuning a Skewed-Blade
Rabbet Block Plane

1 A new skewed-blade rabbet block plane after a few strokes on sandpaper mounted on a granite block. The light areas in this photo are are the high areas that have contacted the sand-paper: behind the throat under the blade where pressure of the lever cap has pushed the area down, a small area at the front of the plane, and another small area at the upper right of the photo (three points make a plane—no pun intended). No part of the sole of the plane at the mouth is making contact, limiting the ability to get a very fine shaving.

2 After about three minutes of sanding. The light areas in this photo are where the sole is not contacting the sandpaper and are still hollow. In order to get the finest shaving, the area at the throat must contact the sandpaper.

Tuning a Skewed-Blade Rabbet Block Plane *(Continued)*

3 After checking that I had not gone out of square to the sides, another three minutes or so on the sandpaper brought the sole into flat. This is sanded to 320 grit.

4 Rather than putting a square on the plane, the better way to check for square is to lay the plane on its side. Unlike the sole, the sides can be "generally" flat with some low spots, as long as the side is flat enough to reference as square when laid on the work. Look at the line of light between the square and the sole: is it tapered? Can you put the square up against it and all light will disappear? If you think you've got it, work with the plane. If it cuts consistently out of square, then your geometry is off somewhere.

5 Make a template of the blade angle when you first get the plane (and don't lose it over the years!). This will help you later when you find that after many sharpenings your blade angle is off and you want to adjust it.

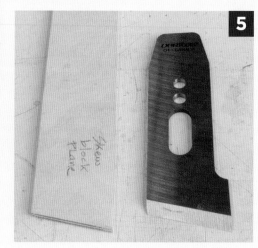

6 Now the sides and sole are square and the blade is adjusted parallel to the sole—but the mouth opening is not parallel to the blade. This means (a) the blade bed is not square to the sides because it was either milled that way, or I managed to take more off one side of the sole than the other and then sanded the sides square to the new sole plane; or (b) the mouth edge is not at the correct angle. Don't correct for (a); file the mouth opening until it is parallel to the blade (when the blade is parallel to the sole). This plane has an adjustable throat plate, so remove it for filing.

7 The mouth edge has been filed parallel to the blade edge. If you are interested, a more thorough treatment on preparing metal planes can be found in my book *Getting Started with Handplanes*.

FIGURE 4-13. Check the alignment of the sides of the sole with a straight edge.

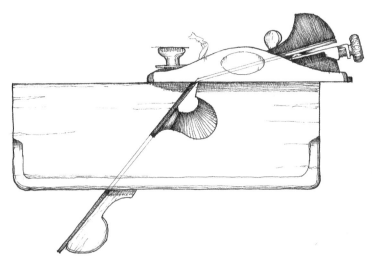

FIGURE 4-14. It can be helpful to take a light plane stroke off the sole behind the blade, as this area is under a lot of pressure and may flex down and hold the blade off the work, preventing it from cutting.

I have fewer reservations about straightening and squaring up a wood rabbet plane, as the wood is much easier to work and it will probably need it periodically anyway. In addition to flattening the sole, make sure both sides are straight (they tend to get pushed out of line around the blade) as well as square to the sole (**Figure 4-13**). Remember when flattening the sole to put the blade in place at full operating pressure, about 1/16" (2mm) shy of the sole. On the traditional wood rabbet planes open on both sides, the blade bed is supported only by the bulk of wood behind it and so pushes the sole down behind the blade a greater amount than many other planes. After planing the sole flat, you can then place the plane's blade behind the mouth of the rabbet plane. Take one or two light strokes off the area behind the blade to lower it a fraction more (**Figure 4-14**).

Sometimes, the traditional wood rabbet plane is badly twisted with the area in front and behind the blade badly misaligned. Straightening this up with a plane might remove too much wood. You can remedy this by cutting a portion of the sole off and re-gluing a continuous piece back on. After the glue has set, the blade bed and mouth opening can be cut back in. This also gives you the chance to cut a new, tighter mouth opening (**Figures 4-15A, 4-15B, and 4-15C**).

FIGURE 4-15A. To straighten a twisted sole, you can cut a portion of it off, usually just to the depth of the bevel of the blade (so you don't have to re-bed the blade), and glue a continuous piece back on. When the glue is dry you can cut the mouth opening tight to the blade and finish cutting the opening by cutting the waste away at the blade seat. Come back and finish paring the blade seat to match the existing configuration.

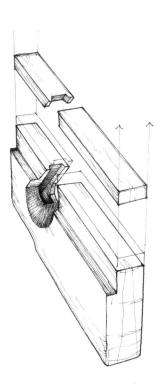

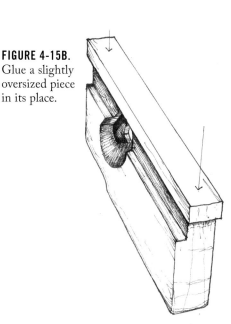

FIGURE 4-15B. Glue a slightly oversized piece in its place.

6. Adjust the Mouth

On a metal rabbet plane with a fixed mouth, you are stuck with what you get. Correcting a badly formed or abused mouth will be unproductive, and closing it down will not be possible. On a plane with an adjustable mouth, you can, of course, adjust the mouth tighter. Just make sure the parts stay in alignment when they are moved (though this is going to be tough to correct if these parts are not milled right). On a wood rabbet plane without an adjustable mouth, you can repair it as described above for fixing a twisted sole—or you can live with it. If you find you need a plane that can make a more finished cut, you will have to upgrade to a plane with a tighter mouth, an adjustable mouth, a chipbreaker, or two of these three.

FIGURE 4-15C. Trim the piece straight and to the width of the blade. Project a line for the blade seat and the blade edge, and cut the opening.

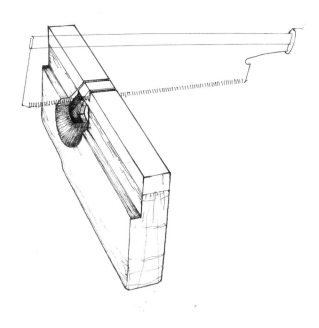

7. Attend to the Details of the Body and Sole

Rabbet planes have a strong tendency to jam with chips (the bench- and block-plane styles of these planes have less of this problem). The solution can be as simple as frequently pushing the shaving out the exit hole—sometimes as often as every stroke of the plane. This can become a little annoying, but if you forget to do it, the consequence is worse: the shavings become tightly jammed, and clearing them entails a prolonged struggle. It becomes even more frustrating when you have to do this repeatedly.

On a metal plane, you do not have much recourse, but on a wood one you can open the chip spillway. This is best accomplished by opening one side more than the other in kind of a funnel shape so that the shaving has a tendency to spiral out the side when it hits the chip opening, rather than getting captured and bunching up. You can use a gouge for the initial opening, followed by a small half round rasp and files. You may not be able to actually get it to spiral out the side, but at least it will make the plane easier to clean out. Just do not remove too much wood and weaken the plane.

Restoring a Wood Rabbet Plane

1 The plane as it came from the flea market. Solid, no cracks or beetle holes. The wedge, though, is pretty much not useable. I noticed a waffle pattern of pliers (probably vise-grips) on the end of the wedge, used at some point to try and withdraw it. Probably thanks to their efforts, it was easy enough to get out when I got it.

Restoring a Wood Rabbet Plane *(Continued)*

2 The blade was in pretty good shape; that is, no rust or pitting. Notice the diagonal line where the blade steel ends and meets the backing steel (there's backing steel underneath it as well, of course).

3 The bevel was badly ground, but that is almost to be expected. I don't think I've ever gotten a used blade that was well ground or had a useable edge on it. Notice that the sides of the blade have a back bevel: preserve these if you have to grind the width of the blade.

4 The blade angle doesn't begin to match the skew angle. Notice the nail holes from where fillets have been tacked on to use as a guide for forming rabbets.

5 Checking all faces with a straightedge showed that there was no major twist or misalignment of the sole or sides. Nor was the wear on the sole particularly bad, so this plane could be trued up by flattening and squaring up its surfaces, rather than having major replacement surgery.

6 The first few passes with a plane show that the front of the plane is out of alignment.

7 High spots show up after a few more passes with the plane.

8 As work progresses, check for twist and correct.

9 Side complete.

10 Time to do the other side.

11 The geometry we saw when planing the first side is reflected on the second. The sides must be parallel to each other when done; check frequently by measuring as the work progresses.

12 Side complete for now. After shooting this sequence, I realized that the center portion of the plane was not well supported. Also, if the dog pressure was cranked up (I try to use just enough pressure to hold the work) when in line with the opening of the blade escapement, the plane could be flexed, or even damaged. Luckily the block is pretty rigid, and checking the work showed that everything remained true and flat.

13 First passes with a plane on the sole. I did the initial planing of the sole without the blade in; after a new wedge is made, and the blade wedged up, I can finish truing the sole.

14 Sole planed flat and square—done for now.

15 The blade was ground badly out of alignment with the skew of the escapement. The correct angle was marked with a felt tip for guidance at the grinder. The nail holes can be clearly seen here.

16 A flat has been ground at the edge of the blade to match the angle of the mouth opening. The bevel will then be ground back until this flat just disappears.

17 You can see the flat on the edge of the blade a little better here. After grinding the bevel, I had to grind quite a bit off the side of the blade for it to match the thickness of the body. Match the angles that are on the edges when you grind the width so that there is sufficient relief to clear the work when the plane is being used.

Restoring a Wood Rabbet Plane *(Continued)*

18 After the blade has been ground and honed to the correct angle, a new wedge is made. Trace the angle of the existing wedge and cut a long blank at this angle.

19 Blanks for the wedge cut. Since this is a skewed blade, the edges of the wedge are angled. Transfer this angle from the original wedge to the end of the blank and plane the edges to match. (Be careful to get the angle going the right way; I didn't, and had to use the second blank!)

20 The blank fitted: the taper has been adjusted so that it bears along the entire length of the blade and the wood escapement it bears against.

21 Once fitted, the profile of the wedge is marked and cut. I used another wedge I liked for the profile, which is designed to be able to be tapped both in and out.

22 The blade is wedged in under operating pressure, but back from the sole about ¹⁄₁₆" (2mm), and the sole planed true and square. As a final touch, a couple shavings are taken off the sole just behind the opening under the blade. This will allow you to get the finest shavings.

23 The plane will now make a variety of shavings, including some very fine ones with little or no tearout.

5

Fillister and Moving-Fillister Planes

FIGURE 5-1. A classic, simple moving-fillister plane, the fence is fixed to the bottom of the plane with screws through slotted holes.

Four hundred years ago, an English craftsman was as concerned with making a living as anyone is today. To increase his profit, he standardized his product and minimized his tool investment as much as possible. He might have one rabbet plane that he used for everything, or, more likely, he had one rabbet plane with a fence integral to the body, since he cut only one size of rabbet in his work. In addition, if he cut several sizes, then, for efficiency, he would have several rabbet planes, each one fit with the appropriate fence.

The craftsman faced with making the occasional new or customized product would take his unfenced rabbet plane and tack a small strip of scrap wood, called a fillet, to the bottom of his rabbet plane to make a fence. (This is also the reason the British often retain the original spelling of this type of plane: the filletster plane.) This was not an uncommon occurrence even into the twentieth century. You can still find all sorts of rabbet planes with nail holes on the bottom and sides, evidence of temporary fences having been tacked on. Around three hundred years ago, the toolmakers caught on and started offering a rabbet plane with an adjustable fence (moving fillister) that could cut any size rabbet without having to put nail holes all over the plane. (As it is a bit awkward to use the full title of "moving-fillister plane," I often will be calling them simply fillister planes.)

The fillister plane (**Figure 5-1**) is a "joint-forming" more than a "joint-trimming" plane, and as such will find fewer uses in most modern shops than the unfenced rabbet plane. With the fence and depth stop, they can be rather awkward to use for simple trimming. However, on some of the planes, the fence and depth stop (if provided) can be removed (and reinstalled when needed), allowing the plane to be used more easily for a variety of paring jobs as well.

I do not use my moving-fillister plane nearly as much as my rabbet planes. However, sometimes the piece to be rabbeted is just too big or too awkward to put on the table saw, or, because of balance, access, or size, it is too risky to use the router. Sometimes the assembly sequence precludes cutting a rabbet until after the piece is installed. There may be just too much invested to risk ruining a piece by trying to balance the router on an insubstantial ledge. If you do woodworking for any length of time, you will end up needing a moving-fillister plane.

Besides the fence, which by definition all moving-fillister planes have, they often come with a depth stop and a cutting spur. The depth stop is a useful accessory but is not necessary. For one thing, it is often hard to depend on. Depth stops tend to be small, and often in front or back of the blade. If the plane is tilted out of parallel with the stop's bearing surface, you will get a misreading—usually stopping short of the rabbet's full depth but occasionally cutting slightly deeper. The depth stop is best used as a reference, checking the rabbet's depth when the stop first appears to bottom out. Alternatively, on some planes you can retrofit a larger full-length stop. A full-length stop is more accurate but harder to set up because it must be parallel to the sole. Even then, debris can get between the stop and the work, so you have to check.

More important is having a cutting spur or scoring knife. This speeds the work, because you do not have to score the wood for a cross grain rabbet and then try to get your fence exactly adjusted to the score line. Spurs have a couple of different configurations: one is some form of knife, and the other is more literally a spur—or *nicker*—a small scoring blade that can be rotated when one side gets dull. I prefer the knife form because the spur does get dull, sometimes rather quickly. Though rotation is possible, eventually you will have to sharpen it, and it is not as easy to sharpen. You will have to rig up a holding jig. Some of the knife-type scoring blades are also rounded; these stay sharper a little longer, but are also harder to sharpen than their straight-edged cousins.

I believe a skewed-blade fillister plane with a chipbreaker or adjustable mouth is preferable to a straight-blade fillister for the same reasons a rabbet plane is: the skewed blade can hog wood more easily, but if it also has a chipbreaker or adjustable mouth, it can also do fine smoothing; and it's more effective on cross grain work.

Choosing Your Fillister Plane

There are now a wide variety of fillister planes in both metal and wood. It wasn't that long ago the common, and indeed almost the only, fillister plane was the Stanley #78 and its competitor's variations. Even though I know it is the standard carpenter's plane preferred by generations of craftsman, I could never warm up to the Stanley #78. I find it awkward and uncomfortable, and because it is iron, it presents quite a lot of friction and must be lubricated generously and frequently. Also, the blade is square to the plane, reducing its cross grain effectiveness. It also has no chipbreaker and a rather large throat. Currently and for a few decades previous, the plane has not been well made, requiring quite a lot of work to true it up. The fence also often proving not true or able to hold its adjustment. But it is certainly affordable, so if you're just starting out or are not too demanding of what you want out of the tool, and are willing to put in some time (or get lucky), this might be a suitable tool.

But you certainly have a pretty good selection of fillister planes to choose from now. In metal-body planes, you have both skewed- and square-blade block plane style fillisters, and bench plane style fillisters such as the jack rabbet fillister. You also have Lee

FIGURE 5-2. A Japanese moving-fillister plane with a chipbreaker, scoring knife (or spur), and a brass sole plate to reduce wear. The plane is a solid performer, able to remove large amounts of wood or to be set finely to leave a polished cut. It can also be used across the grain. It has a few idiosyncrasies, however. The maximum width of cut is only 1" (25mm) and at its maximum setting, the wing nuts that tighten the fence can interfere with the work. Remedy the problem by reinstalling their screws so the wing nuts tighten down in an out-of-the-way position. As with many rabbet planes, the chips will pack in the opening right above the blade point. Open the area with a file.

Valley's rabbet planes. In wood-body planes, you can choose from antique planes, E.C. Emerich's fillister plane, and Japanese-style fillister planes (**Figure 5-2**).

The issues in choosing a fillister plane are similar to those used to choose a rabbet plane. If you want only one plane and you need that plane to reliably leave a smooth surface rather than just be able to remove a lot of wood, that plane must have available one, if not all, of the three tactics most important to achieving a tearout-free surface: an adjustable throat, a chipbreaker, and an appropriate blade angle. Such a plane will have maximum utility. The size of the plane must also fit the size of the work you are doing.

Also to be considered is whether the plane has a cross grain cutting spur and a depth stop. The depth stop is handy for repeat work, but really, if you are cutting

FIGURE 5-3. *Veritas skew moving-fillister plane.*

© Lee Valley Tools Ltd.

a lot of rabbets, you should do them on a machine. I find the depth stop requires user input—like every hand tool (notice I didn't say *nearly* every hand tool), it's not to be relied upon blindly. It must be checked. I like to think of it as a reference, as in "now it's time to check the depth." I find many of my hand-cut rabbets are not repeats, so setting the depth stop is time consuming and of questionable reliability. For one or a few rabbets, I often prefer cutting to a scribe line.

I wouldn't let lack of a depth stop keep me from considering some of the more versatile rabbet planes that also have the capability of a fillister, such as one of the rabbet block planes. Also, skewed-blade Japanese fillisters with their high-quality blades and chipbreakers are usually without a depth stop, but are still worth considering. On these planes, a depth stop can easily be retrofitted, though for years I haven't felt the need to do it and have gotten along just fine.

The Lee Valley fillisters are currently one of the best metal rabbet planes

made, having all the advantages—and disadvantages—of iron. But not having a chipbreaker or an adjustable mouth, sooner or later you will run into a difficult piece of wood. If the rabbet shows, you will be forced to clean it up, requiring the use of a second plane (**Figure 5-3**).

Fence Solutions

There are a number of different fence solutions used in these planes. On the Western and Japanese traditional wood moving-fillister plane, the simplest and perhaps the most reliable is the use of a piece of wood attached to the sole with a couple of screws in slotted holes (see **Figure 5-1**). The modern ECE fillister uses a bent metal fence proportionally the same size as this classic wood fence. Perhaps because these fences are rarely deeper than about 5/8" (16mm), not much leverage can be applied in use that can shift the fence. This shallow fence makes it easier to set up work without the fence running into the bench or stops, on the downside, because it doesn't protrude down much. However, it is not useful for helping reference the cut parallel and square to the surface, and you must rely solely on visually positioning the body of the plane properly—but then, you have to do that anyway (**Figure 5-4**).

The second method used on traditional Western wood planes to mount the fence is by mounting rods to the body of the plane. The fence is then fixed by wedging the rods, using double locking nuts, or a bridle clamp attached to the fence that tightens down on rods fixed to the body. I think with the double locking nut system you're going to have the most reliability, but I've had good luck with the wedge system (which is also easiest to DIY when making or modifying a plane).

Metal planes use rods mounted to the body to attach the fence. These are locked in place with set screws or with locking collets. But there is a problem endemic to the metal moving-fillister planes with their fences mounted to rods—even in the new, high-end designs (and some wood ones). Because cutting a rabbet can apply a lot of leverage to the fence, the locking nuts can slip and the fences creep. The Stanley #45 is good at this. While knurling on the nuts implies that finger tightening is sufficient, it often isn't and the nuts must be tightened down with pliers (or a screwdriver, as the case may be). You have to be aware, though, that even then the fence can creep, and keep your eye on it while you work.

Setting Up the Moving-Fillister Plane

All the procedures for rabbet planes apply here. Additionally, you must prepare the fence, scoring knife, and depth stop.

The fence must be straight, square to the sole, able to be made parallel to the side of the plane, and securely fixed. The fence should not flex under normal use. Cast-metal fences are usually tolerably straight, but it does not hurt to check and spend a few minutes sanding yours

smooth. If it is not straight, square, or parallel, you will have to file and then sand it, similar to the instructions given for preparing the soles of metal planes, using scrapers, files, and straightedges.

Whether you need to tune it up or not, the fence should at least be smoothed to 220 or 320 grit and the edges filed and sanded smooth to avoid marring the work. I say "avoid," but it is difficult to keep a metal fence from marring the work. You will have better luck screwing a wood face to the metal fence. Besides being less likely to mar a project, a wood face has other advantages. You can use it to correct an out-of-whack fence because wood is easier to shape (though the best procedure is to do the fence itself). You can make the fence bigger, often

FIGURE 5-4. E.C. Emerich's rabbet and dovetail planes use a small sheet metal fence fixed with two screws, an evolution from the simple wood fence found on older traditional planes. It's reliable in use, but often needs some straightening before it can be put to work.

improving accuracy and stability in use, though a larger fence will also often get hung up on the work, in which case you may want to have several faces of different sizes available. Its extra thickness, however, will reduce the width of rabbet it will be able to cut.

The stamped metal fence and depth stop of the German planes must be looked to as well; sometimes it is bent, and you may have to tap it a bit with a hammer to straighten it before sanding. Check to see that the fence is square to the sole. It is not very deep, and part of its depth has a radius, so it is hard to tell. The same is true of the depth stop.

On the German moving-fillister planes, be careful when adjusting the blade. If it descends too far, it will contact the metal fence and nick the blade. The underside of the fence is relieved, but only slightly, so you do not have much play.

Depth stop designs vary. The most important thing is to make sure its contact surface can be made parallel to the sole, and it locks securely. A bit of rounding to the infeed and outfeed edges of the depth stop is a good idea (if it has not been done already), as it can help prevent marring of the work.

The nicker (or spur) or scoring knife should be flush with the side of the plane. If it is not, shim it with paper to bring it flush. If it protrudes too far, on a wood rabbet plane carefully pare a little wood away from under the scoring knife. On a metal plane, if it is not adjustable, you will have to hone some off the back of the knife. Sharpen the scoring knife, but do not hone the back any more than you have to, as taking away metal here (on a nicker that can't be adjusted) affects the alignment with the side of the plane.

Using the Moving-Fillister Plane

When using a fillister plane without a spur, the blade is adjusted ¹⁄₆₄" (0.4mm)—or less—beyond the side of the plane. If you are using a fillister with a spur, adjust the blade even with the spur to start and the spur slightly deeper than the blade set. If your spur is nice and sharp and the point of your blade crisp and sharp as well, this should work. But if the condition of your spur or blade is less than optimal and the wood hard or resilient, you may have to extend the blade ever so slightly beyond the spur, as described in the section on rabbet planes. A few test cuts on scrap can help you sort this out.

Measure the width of the rabbet from the spur—which essentially is the side of the plane (not the edge of the blade). Measure at each fixing point of the fence to ensure that the fence is parallel to the sole. If your fence has only one fixing point, be aware you can probably flex the fence if you bear down on it, causing inconsistent results.

When making a cross grain rabbet with a fillister plane, draw the plane backward at least once to get a clean score line that completely cuts the top fibers. Make sure the fence is in solid contact with the work when you do this, because it is easy to tilt the plane, score a line beyond the rabbet, and mar the work.

With the exception of Japanese fillisters and Lee Valley's skew block plane and jack rabbet plane, fillisters have neither chipbreaker nor mouth adjustment. This makes stock selection and grain orientation an important consideration, especially if the rabbet shows. But regardless of whether you have the ability to do this in your project, the cut is started at the end of the board your cutter faces (i.e., the far end with a push plane, the near end with a pull plane). Start with a cut less than the length of the plane, with each succeeding cut a similar length until you reach the end of the board. Repeat this, maybe with longer strokes, several times until the cut is well established. Check that the shoulder is not stepping out and that the bottom is parallel with the main surface. Correct these if necessary: first check your blade adjustment. Make sure that the blade is both parallel to the sole (because you can be holding

The Sash Fillister and Grain Direction

There is a variation on the moving-fillister plane called a sash-fillister plane. The usual moving-fillister plane has the fence on the opposite side of the edge of the blade that cuts the rabbet so you can cut neatly into the edge of any width board. The sash-fillister plane has its fence on the same side as the side of the blade that cuts the shoulder of the rabbet. This means that the width of the piece that can be rabbeted is limited to the span of the rods that hold the fence. This is not a problem, as this is a specialized plane meant to cut the rabbet in window sash, which is rarely thicker than 2" (50mm) or so.

Why not just use a regular fillister plane to cut the rabbet? Well, there are two reasons. The first is that handmade work is always referenced off one side, as when handplaning the thickness, there is always going to be some slight variation. All work is thus referenced off the "show" side, which in this case will be the molding side of the sash so that the molding itself does not show any variation in width.

The second reason is the important point I want to make about all these planes—rabbet, molding, plough, hollows, and rounds. Mostly these planes have no chipbreakers or tightly fitting mouths, so they have no way to control tearout should they encounter gnarly wood. Though many of the molding planes and hollows and rounds had higher cutting angles, often as high as 65°, in an attempt to reduce tearout, mostly what was done was to carefully choose the pieces of wood and orient its grain so that the plane was always cutting with the grain, not into it. On window sash, the grain will be oriented to favor the molding side; turning the stile or rail around to cut the rabbet for the glass then from the opposite side with a rabbet plane would result in the plane cutting into the grain and possibly chewing up the work. Progress is thus slower, the work is harder, and the results not as good as if you had worked with the grain.

Many of these joint-making planes are tearout-prone. Stock should be carefully chosen and the plane used with short strokes, moving the cut back only about half the length of the plane as you go.

the plane perpendicular but the blade might be out of alignment) and correctly positioned to the side of the plane.

If you find your rabbet has stepped out after you have cut it, you have a couple of options. If you are not too far along, you can readjust the blade to where it should have been (projecting ≤ 1⁄64" [0.4mm]), and then, keeping the fence tightly on the work, take repeated light cuts. The point of the blade will just cut into the work, removing what it should have the first time. It is a bit frustrating, but often most accurate if you can keep the fence on the work. Also, check the alignment of the fence. If it is not parallel to the sole, it can hold the plane off the line. Measure at both fixing points and reset as necessary. If your plane has only a single rod and fixing point (such as the Stanley has), check that the fence is parallel to the sole. If it is not, you probably will not be able to make it parallel. You can add a wood face to the factory fence and make it parallel.

Alternatively, you can correct a stepped-out rabbet by turning the plane on its side and squaring up the shoulder of the rabbet. You can reset the fence so it does not exceed the score line or just eyeball it to the score line. If you did not reset the blade before you started this, however, the blade will step out in the other direction, resulting in a mess remaining in the corner. Then you will have to use the first technique—even more difficult when you get to this point. On occasion, it may be easier to clean up the shoulder with a side-rabbet plane, but make sure the point does not set below the bottom of the plane or you will repeatedly score the rabbet, and the plane will resist cutting sideways.

Once you've established the cut, checked for square, and corrected it if necessary, you can continue cutting the rabbet, checking every few strokes that it remains square. Check that the bottom of the rabbet is parallel to the scribe line or face of the board if you're not using a scribe line. Bring the bottom into parallel by using short strokes to lower the high spots, and then long, continuous strokes until you reach your depth.

Controlling the plane and keeping it parallel and square can be difficult. Position your body over the plane so you can sight down it and check that it is setting perpendicular, and not tilted. Use your forehand to keep the fence against the work, and your backhand to push. It helps to use an open hand to push the handle rather than a full grip around the handle, which seems to want to tilt the plane.

6

Plough and Dado Planes

FIGURE 6-1. The classic traditional wood plough plane.

A plough (or plow) plane cuts a groove *with* the grain. It has a fence, which is usually adjustable, and to the casual observer it looks like a moving-fillister rabbet plane. While I'm sure that in some point in its early development there were planes with fixed fences and only one blade width, the plane has for at least a couple hundred years had a moveable fence and the capability of using blades of different widths. It usually has a depth stop, but not scoring blades.

If it has scoring blades, it is a dado plane, whether or not it has a fence. A dado plane is used for making grooves *across* the grain. For this reason it differs from the plough plane in that it has these cross grain nickers (spurs, scoring blades) to score the wood ahead of the cutter so the shoulders of the cut are not splintered at the surface. It has a depth stop but traditionally rarely has a fence, as the plane is often used to cut grooves across the width of long boards like you might make in the sides of a bookcase to support the shelves. A fence would be impractical in this situation, so a scrap of wood (a fillet) is nailed or clamped across the board to guide the plane. Unlike wood plough planes, the wood dado plane, because of the difficulty of aligning spurs with different width blades in a wood body, usually only cuts one width, so if you were doing a variety of work, you might want a set of them.

As metal plane design advanced, "combination" planes were developed that could cut not just variable plow cuts, but also variable widths of dados. These had fences (removable), depth stops, cutting spurs, and a variety of blade widths. Eventually they came with some molding cutters as well. These became increasing complex over the years, culminating in the Stanley #45 and then the #55. Stanley also made simpler versions, such as the #41. More recently, Record had their 050 (**Figure 6-2**). Most recently, Veritas has introduced their version of a combination plane.

Plough and dado planes don't fit my style of work, nor am I particularly enthusiastic about them. And yet I find I actually own four of them—two of which I have used and could probably not have done the job without them. And yet, why did it take two different planes of the same type to do basically the same job?

The two that I have used are a now discontinued Record 050C I bought new back in 1979, and a small Japanese plow, also bought new. The main reason I got the Record was for architectural restoration work: it is almost the only way to cut series of reeds or flutes on a board's surface further from the edge than a router bit's shank is long. All the caveats of timber selection, grain orientation, and technique apply to this tool. The grip is awkward and the settings slip, often widening the cut,

and it is easy to tip the plane in use. Alignment of all the parts is serviceable (most of the time), though borderline. The plowed groove often has rough sides and torn edges even with cutting spurs. I have not tried a cross grain dado cut. Unlike the older dado planes, both wood and metal, the blades are square to the work and not skewed, so the cut is going to be rough.

The other plough plane I use is the Japanese plane, and I use it for cutting $\frac{3}{32}$" (2.4mm)–wide grooves on projects where I don't trust an electric router. It works quite nicely. It has two spurs and a fence, which is not easily removable, so while it will cut nicely across the grain, I can't do it very far from the edge (**Figure 6-3**).

At one point I bought a larger antique Japanese plough plane mainly because it is so instructional. The plane

FIGURE 6-2. The Record 050C Combination plane, able to cut rabbets, grooves, dados, beads, and flutes.

is usually used to cut the tracks for *shoji* sliding doors. Because the door tracks must be smooth so that the doors operate correctly, this plane has not only a chipbreaker to help smooth the bottom of the cut, but also two side cutting blades riding on top of the blade that are used to shear the side walls as the cut progresses. You might think that this is a dado plane because of the side cutters, but these cutters are adjusted at or slightly behind the blade so they would not be effective for eliminating splintering in cross grain work. These side cutters are adjustable not only to align them correctly, but also to compensate for wear from sharpening. It has an adjustable fence and a fixed depth stop. Simple and yet sophisticated.

Unlike the Record, each of the Japanese planes only cuts one size of groove.

FIGURE 6-3. A small Japanese plow plane used for cutting ³⁄₃₂" (2.4mm)–wide grooves. It has two spurs and a fence, so it can cut nicely across the grain.

Using the Plough and Dado

The same techniques are used for the plough plane as are used for the fillister plane: wood selection, making the cut in short passes starting at the far end of the cut (at least until the cut is well established), using the forehand to maintain pressure on the fence against the work and vertical position, and the backhand pushing the plane with an open hand or with a light grip to keep the plane from leaning as it works. Make sure your fence is parallel and set to the correct distance.

If you are doing multiple pieces, it is a good habit to check the fence adjustment before you start each piece, as it may have slipped. An established groove will direct the plane once there's some depth (kind of). When starting a new groove, though it will cut at the new fence position. Keep your eye on the plane as you work; if you find you are leaning and you correct the plane's position and the fence no longer contacts the work, then the fence has slipped its adjustment. If you're doing grooves for a panel in a door, for instance, by the time you do the fourth piece and put it together, the groove may not line up with the first groove. Nothing like spending 20 minutes making firewood.

When the depth stop prevents the plane from cutting, you should be done. It's important to note that historically when you made grooves with a plough plane, they didn't need to be perfectly accurate. These grooves were usually used to hold panels that needed space for expansion and contraction, so small variations in depth were tolerated. However, if the depth of your grooves must be exact, say a joint shows, or must be tight enough to be glued—or both— follow up with a router plane to achieve that accuracy.

With the dado plane, you will most likely have to use a guide, as most dados are too far from the edge to use a fence. You can tack scrap as a fence if you're doing paint-grade work, but otherwise you will have to clamp a straight edge. The plane is drawn backward at least once so the spurs can score the grain. Then the cut is begun at the far side of the groove in short strokes, similar to the plough, until the cut is established, or finished. If the dado tears up at the edges, then the spurs are not aligned with that side of the blade, set in too far, or they are not set deep enough (or both).

7

Shoulder Planes

FIGURE 7-1. Classic shoulder planes are made in this style by both Lie-Nielsen and Clifton.

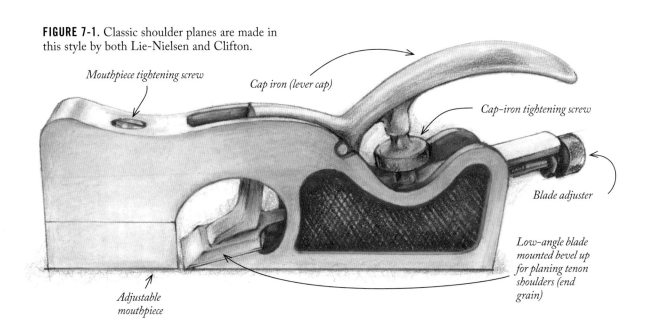

Mouthpiece tightening screw

Cap iron (lever cap)

Cap-iron tightening screw

Blade adjuster

Low-angle blade mounted bevel up for planing tenon shoulders (end grain)

Adjustable mouthpiece

A variant of the rabbet plane, often called and used as such, the shoulder plane (**Figure 7-1**) is distinguished from the basic rabbet plane in that its blade is bedded at a low angle with the bevel up. This setup makes it easier to plane end grain—of the shoulder of a tenon, for instance, which was its original task. Its body is tall in proportion to its width for both visual as well as physical reference to the work. In trimming a tenon shoulder, the shoulder plane is put tight to the tenon to keep the shoulder square to the tenon face (**Figure 7-2**). In addition, the plane can be flipped to trim the adjacent tenon face and can be used to make or trim rabbets. It has no scoring knife or fence.

Just a few years ago, these planes had almost disappeared. Trimming tenon shoulders had evidently dropped far down the modern woodworker's to-do list. However, more recently, woodworkers have begun to realize how versatile and useful shoulder planes can be. The Record #311, 3-in-1, shoulder plane was the second professional plane I got (around 1977), pretty much out of necessity. It has solved a lot of problems for me over the years. Now we have a good selection of well-made and thought-out models available for purchase. I might not have said this a few years ago, but now I believe that if you were to get only one rabbet plane, consider buying a shoulder plane. I recommend the Veritas at ¹¹⁄₁₆" (17mm) wide, so you can also use it in a ¾" (19mm) dado, or a ²³⁄₃₂" (18mm) dado

FIGURE 7-2. When trimming a tenon shoulder, using a bench hook to back up the cut can speed the work and improve accuracy. A board ripped to the thickness of the bench hook can be used to support longer stock.

cut for plywood, as well as to clean up and adjust rabbets.

Traditionally, woodworkers used shoulder planes mostly just on tenon shoulders (seriously—it shows you how important the mortise and tenon joint is!) and other planes for other rabbet-related tasks. The traditional shoulder plane did not have an adjustable mouth. Clifton's shoulder planes, which are beautiful copies of traditional forms that have been in production for a long time, do not have an adjustable mouth. The newer planes, however, such as those from Lie-Nielsen and Veritas, are designed for greater versatility and all have an adjustable mouth. Stanley has remade the #92, and the old #93 and #94 can still be found. While those planes have the theoretical ability to adjust the mouth of the plane to improve the cut and the plane's versatility, the machining on these has been poor, and adjusting to a tight, crisp mouth has been difficult to achieve. The recently introduced and revised version of the #92, however, has received good reviews.

Using the Shoulder Plane

I find an adjustable mouth feature desirable, though not critical. It allows you to quickly and easily reduce tearout, should you need to make a finishing cut. Though a plane might have an adjustable mouth, you should check a few things, if you can, before you buy:

- Can the mouth be closed down an effective amount?

- Is the mouth crisp and well formed?

- Does the plane go out of alignment when the mouth is readjusted?

As with all rabbet planes, the blade must be wide enough to have a minute projection on the cutting side. As both sides of the shoulder plane are used, you must be able to get this projection on both sides of the plane at once. The new, high-quality manufacturers of these planes seem to have the correct blade width. On an older or cheaper plane, however, you may have a mismatched or poorly ground blade and it may step out when cutting a rabbet, or is unable to reach to the inside corner. If the blade is a fraction too narrow, you can always adjust the blade over to that one side a little more. Since the blade, blade's sides, and plane body are square and parallel to one another, this will probably throw

the blade edge out of parallel to the sole. If the blade cannot be made parallel to the sole with an equal amount projecting on either side (assuming the blade edge is honed square and the plane's sole is square to its sides), and the plane steps out in the cut, I would return the plane (or maybe attempt to replace the blade), because there is not enough blade width. On the other hand, with a new plane, there should be no need to grind down excessive blade width. (Setting up a shoulder plane follows many of the same procedures as a rabbet plane; see page 65.)

Another thing I do not suggest you attempt is straightening or squaring the sole and sides of these planes. It is too difficult and there is no way you can improve upon them. If your metal plane is out of square, you need to get a new plane.

Assuming everything is in square, one thing you can do, however, is check the flatness of the sole along its length. Because of the low angle of the blade, there is very little mass under there. This is compounded by the fact that this area is usually the exact place the lever cap applies pressure to keep the blade in place. This will often cause the part of the sole under the blade to deflect and make it difficult to get a very fine shaving. You can check this by backing the blade off so it doesn't project below the sole, adjusting the lever cap so that there is only enough pressure to keep the blade from shifting and no more (this usually isn't very much), and holding the plane up to the light and with a straightedge to the sole, see if you can see light. If the sole contacts the straightedge at the blade bed area and you can see light at the throat area in front of the blade, then you should flatten the sole. Do this carefully with controlled single strokes, checking every three or four strokes that the sole is not sanded on one side more than the other (you can see this by checking the pattern the sandpaper left on the sole), and that it is still square. It also possible to "rock" the plane from end to end by shifting your pressure on each stroke, taking more off there and rounding the sole a fraction along its length without significantly removing material under the blade's bed. Focus your pressure at the plane's center at the blade area. Once the sandpaper leaves its mark all across the throat area in front of the blade (**Figure 7-3**), you can stop. Adjust the blade and take a shaving; you should be able to get nearly see-through shavings. If you later readjust your plane (I think that if you are not using your plane for long periods it is a good idea to back the pressure off a bit) and the plane doesn't cut, then you know you have cranked the pressure down too hard and it should be backed off.

During use, most of these planes, being iron, develop a lot of friction and benefit from frequent light lubrication. Also, on all of these planes, the throat, which is open on the sides rather than the top, captures the shaving, and after about 5' (1.5m) of rabbet, the chipwell loads tight, so you will have to clear the

FIGURE 7-3. I put my Clifton 3110 on the sanding platten and a few passes showed that it was making contact all across the mouth, some behind it and at the heel of the plane as well as the toe, not continuous but sufficient along its length. Done.

shavings frequently. Also beware: It is easy to crank the blade-clamping screw down too tight; not only do you depress the bed of the plane enough to stop it from cutting, but you can crack the casting, either at the bed or at the lever cap's pivot point (a friend of mine broke his plane by doing this).

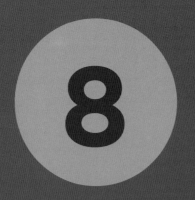

Bullnose and Chisel Planes

FIGURE 8-1. The Clifton 3-in-1 plane disassembled: chisel plane, bull-nose piece, and rabbet-plane nosepiece.

FIGURE 8-2. The Clifton 3110 3-in-1 plane in its bullnose configuration.

The most common versions of the bullnose and chisel planes are variations of the shoulder rabbet plane. In some cases, the variations actually are a shoulder rabbet plane that disassembles into a bullnose or chisel plane (**Figure 8-1**). There are a few uncommon versions that are essentially modified bench planes that cannot reach into the corner of a rabbet. By far the most useful, however, are variations of shoulder rabbet planes, so I will confine my comments to these.

A bullnose plane has a short nose, that is, minimal area in front of the blade, usually about ¼" (6mm) so it can work in close to inside corners and other restricted areas. A chisel plane has no nose—the blade projects unobstructed

for working right into corners. These are not necessary tools in the kit of many woodworkers. I advise waiting until you need one before buying. When you do need one, though, nothing works quite as well (**Figure 8-2**).

Using Bullnose and Chisel Planes

These planes have limited use outside the tasks for which they were designed. The bullnose plane works okay for general planning of rabbets, but its short nose makes it harder to start, and, along with the plane's overall short length, reduces its stability and accuracy. It is more difficult to use than a regular rabbet plane. In addition, the chisel plane is nearly impossible to use. Removing the sole in front of the blade removes the bearing area that resists the tendency of the blade—and the whole plane—to dive into the cut. Only the greatest concentration on keeping the sole on the work and taking the lightest of cuts will yield anything approaching satisfactory results.

If you need to adjust or smooth a stop rabbet, you will have to use the bullnose and chisel plane in combination to work into the corner. You can plane the majority of the rabbet with a standard rabbet plane (probably faster) or the bullnose, as far into the corner as the front of either plane will allow. Switch to the bullnose (if you've used the standard rabbet) to get within ¼" (6mm) of the corner. You will be able to do only two or three strokes before the plane stops cutting because the front of the sole is riding up on the uncut portion. Then you will have to switch to the

chisel plane to finish into the corner, and then go back and repeat the process. Alternatively, you can start with the chisel plane and work back out from the corner with the bullnose and rabbet planes. The process is the same either way.

You will have a better time of it if you can match the bullnose and chisel planes stroke for stroke so you do not end up cutting the depth of two or three shavings at one pass with the chisel plane—it is difficult enough to use for single shavings. However, few of us can justify having both a bullnose and a chisel plane and must therefore assemble and disassemble our combination bullnose/chisel plane to accomplish this task. If you have a lot of wood to remove, it is often faster to chisel down close to the depth you want to achieve in the corner for at least the length of the nose on the plane. The bullnose plane can work all the way to the corner, and finish into the corner with just a shaving or two with the chisel plane or paring chisel.

9

The Router Plane

Say you have just cut a dado on the table saw across a somewhat large panel. Upon trial assembly you discover the depth is not consistent because of the difficulty of keeping a large panel down tight to the saw table. If you put it back on the table saw, you risk coming off the fence. Even if you do not, cutting a dado a second time usually widens it, ruining the fit. If you have cut the dado with a router, you risk widening that, too, if you re-cut it. The safest and most expedient solution is the router plane (**Figure 9-1**). Its small base, about the size of a router, will follow the surface of the panel closely, resulting in an accurate depth without risk of cutting the sides of the dado.

Before power tools, the router plane was the go-to tool when you wanted to make a recess such as a stopped dado in a cabinet side for shelves or the recess for stair treads and risers in a housed stringer. While the router plane is still useful on occasion for making joints, its main use today is in fine-tuning them.

The plane is made in both wood and metal versions. The traditional wood version, pretty much unchanged for centuries, is still available. Despite its overwhelming simplicity (which is probably its strength), it remains an effective, if limited, tool. It is not a subtle tool, however, having no screw adjustment or accessories like a depth stop. Because of its mass, the wood

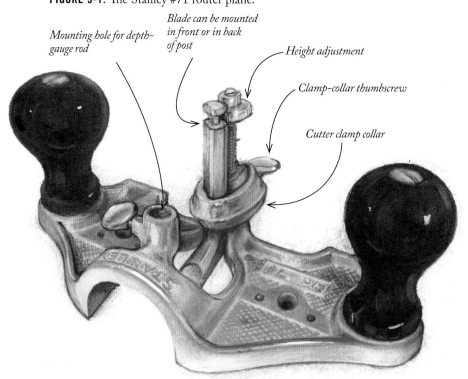

FIGURE 9-1. The Stanley #71 router plane.

Mounting hole for depth-gauge rod

Blade can be mounted in front or in back of post

Height adjustment

Clamp-collar thumbscrew

Cutter clamp collar

version of the router plane's main virtue is the ease with which wood can be removed, especially compared to its metal cousin.

The Stanley #71 Router Plane

For decades the Stanley #71 router plane (and the Record #071) was the only other version available. But Stanley has discontinued its model #71 router plane, though I believe the small #271 (**Figure 9-2**) is still being made. They still can be found rather easily, and earlier versions are also readily available, priced rather affordably since few people know what to do with them anymore. They are all, including the last version by Stanley—which still betrays its nineteenth-century roots—studies in Victorian design concepts. Their function generates flowing lines and edges, and different motifs and textures accenting screws, holes, and housings.

The Stanley #71 came with a number of accessories that were developed over the years because the tool was used for so many different tasks (just think how valuable the power router is today). The most interesting one is a rod that sits in front of the position of the blade (**Figure 9-3**) that can be used to attach a shoe to give the plane more support on narrow work. It is also used as a depth stop, but, I think, not in the way many think it is used. It is often thought that the rod is meant to sit loose in its hole with the shoe screwed to the top part of it as a stop set at a distance equal to

the depth of the cut. In use, the blade is constantly readjusted as the cut gets deeper. When the rod drops into the cut, finally coming to rest on the shoe collar, you have reached depth. This is a far-from-accurate way of working. It's hard to tell when it's bottomed out because it's bobbing up and down from vibration when used, and there's nothing to keep you from setting the blade deeper than the intended depth.

I've done some experimenting and I believe (and according to the original instructions—it always helps to read the instructions!) it is used rather as a depth of cut limiter, restricting the thickness of shaving you can make on each pass of the plane, much like the function of the sole of a bench plane. The blade depth is

FIGURE 9-2.
The Stanley model #271 router plane is a small plane suitable for detailed work. Its standard cutter is ¼" (6mm) wide.

FIGURE 9-3. The Stanley #71 router plane with the depth-gauge rod mounted in front of the blade. The rod does not set the final depth of cut; the blade depth does that. When the rod is used, the blade is not readjusted between passes but rather is set to its final depth from the beginning. Functioning more like the infeed table of a power jointer, the rod limits only the amount the blade can shave off with each pass.

set once, repeated passes are made, and when the blade stops cutting, you have reached your desired depth of cut. This speeds the work, as the blade doesn't have to be repositioned after each pass. The cutter can be left at its setting for a series of dados, such as a stair housing, for instance (once, one of its main jobs). This feature works okay for grooves and dados, but for something like relieving the background of a carving, unless you proceed very consistently, it soon gets hung up on the rough surface. The rod will hit the borders of the work before the blade, making it more difficult to cut all the way to the edge.

As I said earlier, this rod also receives a shoe, a sort of sole plate in front of the blade, set flush with the sole to provide support on narrow pieces. The piece is needed because the large arch where the depth stop attaches leaves a gap in the sole, which would make it otherwise unusable on edges. With the depth stop rod allowing the plane almost continual use, I'm supposing it is there for chip clearance, as I imagine they could pile up against the blade, sole, and post pretty quickly. The Stanley #71½ does not have the arch (nor the depth-gauge accessories), so we won't know if this is the case, but it is easier to use on narrow pieces.

Using a Router Plane: Making a Housing for Treads and Risers in a Stair Stringer

Routing out tread and riser housings in a stair stringer was one of the major jobs the router plane was used for. Even for a shallow housing, that's a lot of wood to remove, and it was often done in hardwoods, such as oak. I've removed large areas of wood with the router plane, and I'll tell you that if you have to readjust the blade on every pass, it's slow going indeed.

However, I've since discovered the use of what I now call the "limiter rod" (called the "depth gauge rod" in the original instructions—which I finally decided to read). This allows you to set the blade depth once and keep it there no matter what stage of the work you are at on multiple housings. The rod limits how thick a shaving can be on each pass until the blade reaches full depth and stops cutting. Brilliant!

It does require some user input, though. You must start at the far side of the cut and work toward yourself, removing all material in a pass until the end. If you are inconsistent, a rough surface will hold up the rod and slow you down. Don't set the cut too deep; it makes it harder to get consistent results.

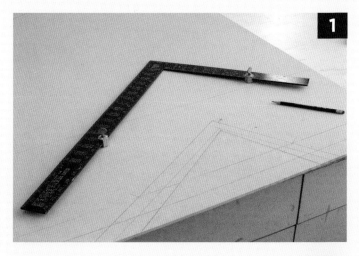

1

1 Good-quality, traditional stairs had "housed stringers," that is, treads and risers were let into dados cut into the stringer (the diagonal board that gets mounted to the wall). The dados were cut ¼" to ½" (6 to 13mm) deep. Glue was applied to the ends of the treads and risers and inserted into the housing. Wedges, with glue applied, were then driven into a matching taper in the dado from the underside to snug them up. On the best stairs, the housing was dovetail-shape, as were the matching ends of treads and risers and the wedges, making very secure stairs.

The router plane was used to cut the housing. Here, you see the template being made that is used to lay out and cut the housing, in this case a rise of 7:11.

2 The template shows tread and riser thickness and the line of the wedge below. The bottom parallel line is the line of the guide piece that will slide along the bottom of the stringer. The second parallel line is the intersection of the riser and tread.

Using a Router Plane: Making a Housing for Treads and Risers in a Stair Stringer *(Continued)*

3 Here the template is cut out and assembled.

4 The template mounted to the stringer. The outline is traced (not a necessity, just a backup).

5 A hole is drilled first to depth where the nosing will be. This is one reason why traditional steps had semicircular-shaped overhangs—it's an easy way to do a stopped cut.

6 The hole is drilled.

7 A dovetail saw, dado saw, or stair saw (all the same saw, two different handle shapes) is placed along the template, and kerfs are made to guide the saw once the template is removed.

8 The other cuts are started. The use of a thicker template limits the saw setting, as most dado saws are limited in their depth of cut. This template is ¼" (6mm) thick; my total depth on the dado is ⁵⁄₁₆" (8mm), allowing me to cut a kerf ¹⁄₁₆" (2mm) deep, enough to guide the saw once the template is removed.

9 All cuts have been made. This style of dovetail saw cuts on the pull stroke, about the only Western saw I can think of that does. I made it from a section of old handsaw and cut a bit of "fleam" on the rip teeth; that is, the tips of the teeth are angled to the length of the blade, rather than perpendicular as are rip teeth. This makes a cleaner cut when angled or perpendicular to the grain. The blade is adjustable in depth. It's called a dovetail saw because the shoulders of the handle at the blade are the same angle as my dovetail plane and can be used as a rough visual guide when cutting dovetailed housings, as well as a depth stop.

Using a Router Plane: Making a Housing for Treads and Risers in a Stair Stringer *(Continued)*

10 With the template removed, the cuts can now be finished. The saw blade is adjusted to the desired depth of the housing and the saw will stop cutting when the shoulder contacts the work.

11 Sawing continues.

12 All cuts are finished.

13 Cuts around the nosing are finished off.

14 Some space is cleared at the nosing for the router plane to start.

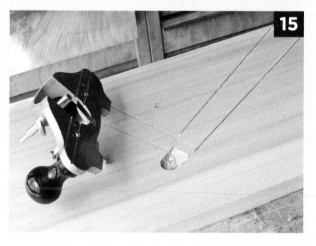

15 The router plane's blade is set to its final depth and the limiter rod is set less than a 1/16" (2mm).

Using a Router Plane: Making a Housing for Treads and Risers in a Stair Stringer *(Continued)*

16 The first cuts are made into the hole of the nosing, then the adjacent cut can be started.

17 The cut is started at the furthest point and progresses toward you. Work consistently; uneven work will leave rough spots that the limiter rod will hang up on, and make the work go slower (and harder).

18 Work back toward yourself. If you are fastidious and keep the chips clear, there will be less marring of the face of the work.

19 A typical housing is complete. If I hadn't stopped to take photos, the router work may have only taken around five minutes. It was so satisfying taking out shavings that I almost forgot to take photos!

Still, I do not like using this plane on narrow edges—to cut a gain for a hinge, for instance, or for the occasional rabbet. The balance is bad because the handles are so far out to the side, making the plane difficult to control and to get a consistent cut. In addition, on short hinge gains, the L-shaped cutter will not be able to cut a gain much shorter than twice its length. The small #271 router plane is easier to balance but has the same problem with blade design that limits how small a gain you can cut. For hardware gains, I prefer using the mortise plane (see page 124).

The plane also came with a fence that could be used on either straight or curved work. It is not very deep, however, and if the final depth of cut is greater than the fence, you will not be able to use the depth-gauge rod, and will have to repeatedly reset the blade as the work progresses. This is not that big of a problem, but because the plane does not have a depth stop, it gets tedious achieving the same depth of cut if you are doing more than one groove.

Other Router Plane Options

Veritas and Lie-Nielsen both now make a router plane to fill the void left by the discontinuation of Stanley's model, and its modern lines reveal the tool's redesign. The most important improvement is the inclusion of an effective depth stop, one that actually holds its adjustment. The depth-gauge rod of the Stanley limits how much wood is removed during each pass while the blade stays fixed. The new depth stop allows the blade to be adjusted up and down, stopping at a fixed depth determined by the stop. Though not as fast as using the rod in forming a

Using the Router Plane

When sharpening the blade, it is hard to keep the sharpened edge square to the blade. If the blade edge is not square, it will not be parallel to the sole of the plane (assuming the plane is manufactured accurately. This is not that critical, because if you consistently pass the blade over all areas of the cut, the low side of the blade will set the depth and the result will be generally consistent. Some minor surface irregularities will remain, depending on how far out of square the edge is. Because most of the surfaces you cut with this plane are hidden, it will not be a problem. Unfortunately, the router plane does not leave a surface ready for finish. Smooth exposed surfaces further with a scraper, and sand as required.

When using the router plane, try not to be too aggressive in setting the depth of cut. You will have a better time of it if you can just shave off a consistent shaving, rather than banging the plane against the cut and taking off the wood in chunks. The Stanley's adjuster has a lot of slop and it tends to bind, so it is hard to advance the cutter consistently, resulting in a cut that is too deep or not deep enough—very often every time you reset the blade. If you have to advance the blade a lot at one time, the locking collar will bind on the Stanley, so you will have to fiddle with that as well.

groove, this is really helpful when you are trimming machine-made grooves and find yourself having to back off the depth of cut for some reason. You may need to work on a set of multiple grooves simultaneously, and then need to finalize them all to an accurate and consistent depth. Having discovered how to use the depth-gauge rod, I believe having both would make the ideal plane. However, because this plane is used more for trimming grooves than for forming them, having the depth stop is probably the more useful accessory.

I have not worked with the Lie-Nielsen, but I have the Veritas router plane. A flange on the adjustment knob engages a groove in the top of the blade stem; this is how the blade is adjusted. The stop, however, haults the adjustment knob, not the blade, so it is quite easy to lock the blade anywhere within the slop of its engagement with the adjustment knob, which is more than $\frac{1}{32}$" (0.8mm). The tolerance on this flange to groove could certainly be tighter—though there's always going to be some play with this setup. Also, this stop

Supplemental Sole

It is not a bad idea on any of the router planes to attach a thin wood sole to the metal sole as a way to reduce the burnishing of the work by the metal sole. The Stanley in particular, even with the sole sanded smooth, still tends to leave marks. Some marring, however, is from minute chips and shavings that get under the sole when using the plane and is unavoidable.

tightens down on the threaded rod that the adjustment knob uses, so while the locking screw is brass and shouldn't hurt the threads, I would expect to see some wear over time. If you pay attention, you can work with this setup and get consistent results, but you really do have to pay attention.

The Lie-Nielsen has a better setup with the depth stop locking onto the blade itself. This is going to make it much easier to get consistent results. I suppose you can still crank the adjustment knob down hard enough to move the stop collar a fraction if you were particularly heavy-handed, or get shavings under it. It's still a better way, though.

The Veritas comes with a spear point blade, a classic accessory that I've never had luck using, and a fence (which I think is of limited use). It also comes with a sharpening system for the ½" (13mm) blades that is genius and a nice touch, none of which are available standard on the Lie-Nielsen. Does this compensate for the sloppy stop system on the Veritas? You decide.

The Veritas also has a longer and deeper fence than the Stanley, though using the fence is more precautionary than necessary. Because any recess the router plane is used to level must first have its boundaries cut with a chisel or saw, the fence functions more as a rough guide restricting movement. With the two widely spaced handles, it is easy to torque the plane to the fence, causing a misregistration and damage to the sides of the cut.

Using the Router Plane

All the versions of the plane allow repositioning of the blade in four positions. The bullnose position is the most useful, allowing you to work right up to obstructions, such as a cabinet back at a dado in a cabinet side.

When setting up the plane, you should not have to do much more than sharpen the blades. However, check the blade seat, especially on the Stanley, to see that it supports the blade post and does not flex when cutting. On my Stanley, the blade post groove was badly milled. This resulted in the blade post riding on a single high spot that allowed the blade to flex under load despite the restraint of the locking collar, resulting in a cut of inconsistent depth. The blade flexed into the wood on a heavy cut, cutting deeper than it was set. It took me a number of projects to figure it out. Take a file and carefully flatten the post seat area enough to get a good bearing for the post. In addition, on the Stanley you will likely have to smooth the sole (the later ones were sanded, not milled, and then nickel plated), or add a wood sole to reduce burnishing the project (there are screw holes in the base for this). An additional sole, however, will reduce the maximum cutting depth of the plane. A trick some carvers will use is to mount an oversize wood base to the plane to bridge the distance when removing large areas of background.

The plane can also be used to correct tenon checks, though I am not a big fan of doing this. This is done by laying

Using a Bridge Board

Many carvers prefer the router plane for relieving the background of a carving, as switching back and forth from power tools to hand carving can be disruptive. In addition, relieving the work by hand gives the carver a feel for the piece of wood he or she is using. For large areas, you can attach a board to the sole to span the distance.

the piece with the tenon on its side and adjusting the depth of cut of the plane to the correct dimension of the tenon cheek cut. If done correctly, this can be an accurate way of perfecting the fit of tenons. Note that it is really easy on longer and/or narrower tenons (say more than 1½" [38mm] long) to lose registration of the plane's sole on the side of the piece and cut deeper or inconsistently into the tenon. You can improve your accuracy by using short cuts, rotating the cutter portion of the plane around the reference face rather than pushing both handles of the plane. You can also move two work pieces that have the same tenon together to support the freehanging side of the plane, but now you're clamping two pieces down for every side of every tenon—a lot of flipping and clamping. And if your handcut tenons vary significantly, you'll have to back the blade off and then reset it, and now you're back to dealing with that inconsistent depth stop. Oftentimes it is sufficient and faster to just work with a rabbet plane holding the piece against a stop.

10

Side-Rabbet Planes

FIGURE 10-1. Stanley #79 and two versions of Japanese-style side-rabbet planes, used to trim the side of a rabbet.

We've got fillister, plow, dado, and router planes to cut rabbets and grooves and smooth and correct their depth, but what if the grooves and rabbets are not wide enough?

This is the function of the side-rabbet plane. These rather unusual looking planes (you might not recognize them as planes at first) are for exactly that: widening the sides of grooves. They are useful for the same reason the router plane can be useful; sometimes it is just too difficult or risky to return to the work with a power tool. A couple passes with one of these can solve the problem of a too-tight groove. In addition, like a number of tools in this book, no other tool does this job as well.

Three forms of this plane remain: the discontinued Stanley #79; the right and left pair called the Stanley #98 and #99, now made by Lie-Nielsen (with a revised combo version made by Veritas); and the Japanese side-rabbet plane, whose solution to the problem is slightly different from the Stanley's (**Figure 10-1**).

The Stanley #79 side-rabbet plane was, for a while, the only Western-style rabbet plane being made (I think it is now out of production; you will have to find a vintage model). It is an awkward little plane to use and to adjust. It does work, though, and it has some features that indicate it has been given some thought over the years. In addition, it is affordable.

The blades are hard to adjust, but once you get them set, you probably will not have to readjust them again soon (you may use this plane so rarely you seldom ever have to resharpen the blades). More than likely there will not be enough room in the blade escapement to align the blades so the edges are both parallel to the bearing surface (the side) and do not project below the bottom of the plane. If the blade projects below the bottom of the plane and you cannot adjust it up any further, you should grind off the point of the blade to make sure that it can be made flush to or only very slightly projecting from the bottom of the plane. Otherwise, the plane tends to hang up on the projecting point, making planning the side more difficult.

This plane has a depth stop and also has a chisel-plane feature, but you will have to remove the depth stop to access the screw that holds the nosepiece. The plane has many sharp, unfriendly areas, and the grip is awkward (at least to me, so far). In addition, the short nosepiece (essentially a "bullnose") makes it difficult to start a cut. The easiest way to start a cut is to put the plane someplace in the groove (as opposed to the end) and trim a side going one way until the cut exits. Then finish the side by putting the plane back in the groove where you started and going the other way until the cutter exits. This doesn't work, however, if this a cross grain cut, in which case you will splinter out on exiting the cut. You will then be forced to try starting the cut balancing on that ¼" (6mm)–long nosepiece. If the grain is gnarly, or directional, this plane will tear out. You can try to combat that by using different ends to cut in more successful directions, but it's hard getting a smooth, continuous surface doing this.

The Stanley models #98 and #99 that Lie-Nielsen now make are mechanically pretty much the same plane as the #79, except made into two planes (a right and left) that are better constructed and a more ergonomic design. They have a depth stop and a removable nosepiece, and the nosepiece is slightly longer than the #79. Veritas makes their own version of a side-rabbet plane, which looks a bit like a Stanley #98 and #99 combined into one plane. This is friendlier than the #79, with a turtle-back handle that rotates according to which side you're using. They also have removable (but short) nosepieces and a depth stop, as well as a choice of blade steels, either O1 or their powdered metal PM-V11. Both the #79 and Veritas are around half the cost of new #98 and #99.

I have not had the chance to work with the #98 and #99, so I cannot really comment on their efficiency. Mainly, I use my Japanese side-rabbet plane if I have to do any trimming, and I use my #79 if the groove is too narrow for the Japanese plane to fit. The #79 is nice and narrow, so it fits into many tight places.

While the Japanese style of side-rabbet plane may be a challenge to those unfamiliar with Japanese planes (and maybe even to some who are familiar), I find it is more effective and easier to use than its Western counterparts. I like this tool. It is easy to hold, easy to use and adjust, has a high-quality laminated blade with a chipbreaker (sometimes tearout on the side of a groove is not acceptable), has long reference areas both before and after the cut for greater accuracy, and can be modified. I angled the adjacent face of mine to the angle of the dovetail plane I have. The angle allows the plane to fit right to the bottom corner of the dovetail groove, and gives me a decent reference face to assist in holding the plane at the correct angle. As with the other side-rabbet planes, if you are not going to take the time to back up the wood when the plane exits a cross grain cut, you really need a right- and left-hand model. Otherwise, you risk splitting out the wood.

The Japanese side-rabbet plane comes in a few different sizes. The smallest ones have the blade self-wedged into the side of the plane; I have this style in a full-size plane (about 10" [254mm]) for a right-hand cut. I also have a plane for the opposite cut that has a chipbreaker that, unlike many other Japanese planes, doubles as the wedge that holds the blade in position. This means that the chipbreaker must be tapped down close to its final position before you can begin adjusting the blade. If the chipbreaker is not tapped into position, the blade is liable to

Using the #79

When using the Stanley #79, (and the #98 and #99, for that matter), because the short nosepiece does not give you a stable area to start the cut, you are often better off starting the cut in from the end (so you can bear more of the side of the plane on the side of the groove). You continue, running the cut to the far side. And you finish by coming back the other way, cutting the first uncut portion with the other blade (or, in the case of the complementary planes, the other plane). This technique works fine in dadoes with the grain (technically called a plough). However, if you are trimming a cross grain dado, you will be forced to come in from the ends to avoid splintering. You will then have to attempt to get the cut started balancing on that short nosepiece. Also, because of the #79's low profile and awkward ergonomics, it can be difficult to tell if the cut is vertical.

come flying out at the first disturbance, injuring you, the blade, or both. If you interested in exploring this option, you can read more about setting up these planes in my book *Discovering Japanese Handplanes*.

Finally, I discovered that before Stanley, several manufacturers made a wood version of the side rabbet plane. Curiously, it resembles the Japanese version, but I have never seen this plane in person and think that it is pretty uncommon. The blade is rather centrally placed, which would certainly help with starting the cut, pitched at a high angle, the blade slightly skewed to make the cut. It would seem with its high angle both in pitch and skew it would give a scraping cut; this would certainly reduce tearout, but not work so well for end grain. But I haven't had the opportunity to use this plane.

The Dovetail Plane

The dovetail plane (**Figure** 11-1) cuts the male portion of a sliding dovetail, either cross grain or along the grain. It is a moving-fillister plane with its sole angled to its side so that it cuts a 73° or 80° rabbet (a dovetail) rather than a 90° rabbet. The blade is usually skewed, with the leading point on the offside of the cut, unlike the skewed-blade rabbet plane where the leading point is toward the work. This allows the blade to slice with the grain of the rising dovetail V groove on the cross grain dovetail that you might find on the end of a board, used to join a shelf to its standard, for instance. It has, by necessity, a fence and, for cross grain work, a scoring knife. It does not typically have a depth stop because you do not usually need to use one when cutting the male dovetail, which is very often tapered. The planes come in at least a couple of different angles (10° and 17°, usually).

The sliding-dovetail joint is an excellent solution for mounting cross grain battens used to stiffen and keep straight panels and doors. It is a common technique throughout the world. I have seen 500-year-old Chinese tabletops

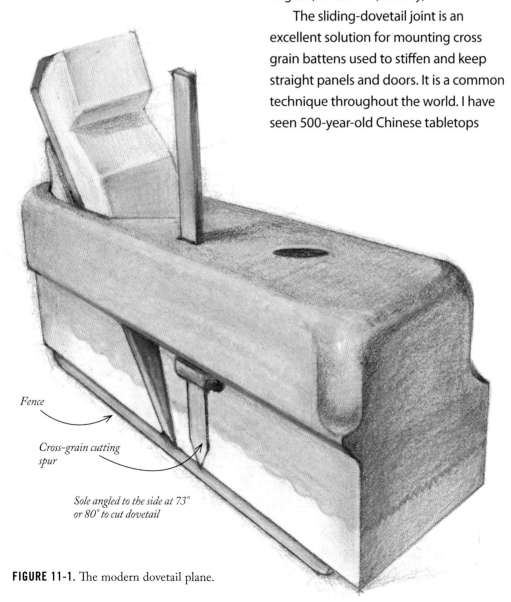

Fence

Cross-grain cutting spur

Sole angled to the side at 73° or 80° to cut dovetail

FIGURE 11-1. The modern dovetail plane.

Sliding Dovetail

The reason it is so difficult to get a sliding dovetail to fit tight is pure geometry. With a 10° dovetail, for instance, removing material perpendicular to the face of the dovetail results in a gap equaling more than five times that amount in a direction perpendicular to the face of the housing. Therefore, if you shaved ¹⁄₁₀₀" (0.25mm) off the face of the dovetail, you would end up with a gap close to ¹⁄₁₆" (2mm) in the direction that would normally wedge the dovetail tight. This is even more dramatic along the length of a tapered

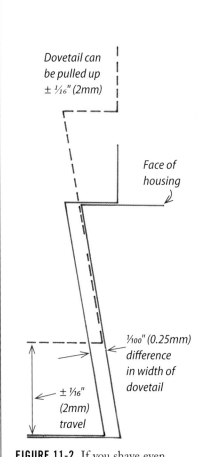

Dovetail can be pulled up ± ¹⁄₁₆" (2mm)

Face of housing

¹⁄₁₀₀" (0.25mm) difference in width of dovetail

± ¹⁄₁₆" (2mm) travel

FIGURE 11-2. If you shave even only ¹⁄₁₀₀" (0.51mm) off the width of a tight-fitting dovetail, it will be loose enough to move a full ¹⁄₁₆" (2mm) apart.

dovetail batten. Because the taper may be only a couple of degrees (or less), a single pass with a dovetail plane may remove enough material to advance the batten a ½" (13mm) or more.

only ⅜" (9mm) thick kept nearly dead flat by the use of a dovetailed batten underneath. Japanese shoji makers use the dovetailed batten to keep the wood panels in doors flat. It is a more effective and definitely more elegant solution than a batten attached with screws through slotted holes. But if you have ever tried to cut and fit a long sliding dovetail, you know how difficult it can be to get a fit both sufficiently tight and yet accurate enough that you can still drive the batten all the way home.

The friction on even a well-cut sliding dovetail is tremendous. One way to make the joint both tighter and faster is to use a tapered, rather than a straight, sliding dovetail. The joint goes together easily, cinching up tight at the last taps. While you can cut both straight and tapered dovetails by machine, the dovetail plane excels at both trimming and making this joint, particularly the tapered dovetail. You can cut and fit tapered dovetails on a number of battens in the time it would take you to make the complicated jig to rout them.

Another occasion when the dovetail plane would be preferable to routing by machine is when the pieces to be dovetailed are too long to easily machine. For instance, the tapered sliding dovetail is an excellent joint for locking the ends of shelves into a carcass.

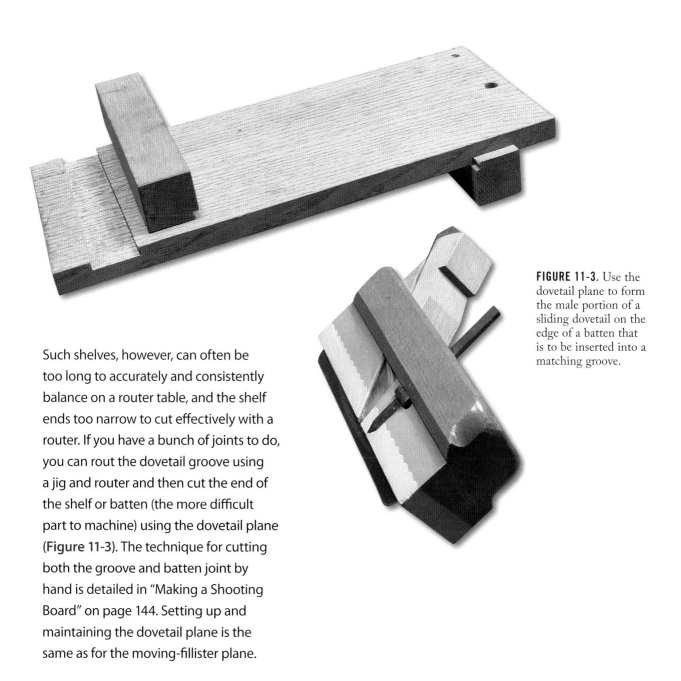

FIGURE 11-3. Use the dovetail plane to form the male portion of a sliding dovetail on the edge of a batten that is to be inserted into a matching groove.

Such shelves, however, can often be too long to accurately and consistently balance on a router table, and the shelf ends too narrow to cut effectively with a router. If you have a bunch of joints to do, you can rout the dovetail groove using a jig and router and then cut the end of the shelf or batten (the more difficult part to machine) using the dovetail plane (Figure 11-3). The technique for cutting both the groove and batten joint by hand is detailed in "Making a Shooting Board" on page 144. Setting up and maintaining the dovetail plane is the same as for the moving-fillister plane.

The Mortise Plane

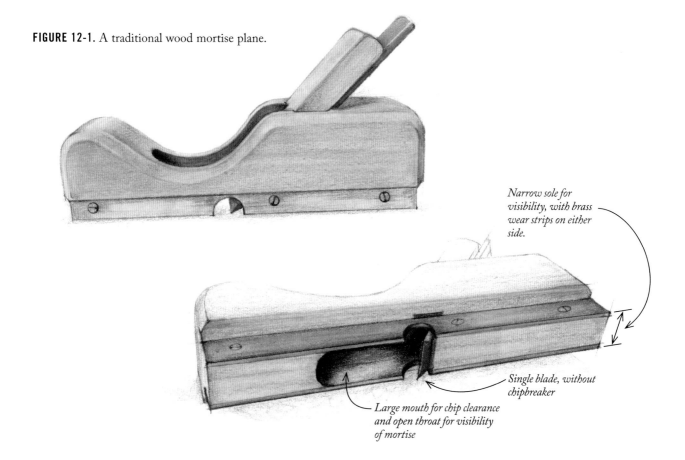

FIGURE 12-1. A traditional wood mortise plane.

Narrow sole for visibility, with brass wear strips on either side.

Single blade, without chipbreaker

Large mouth for chip clearance and open throat for visibility of mortise

The mortise plane (**Figure 12-1**) is not a *must-have*. I got mine out of the clearance bin about 25 years ago for $10 and thought, for that price, I'll give it a try. It has been very useful. I got my money's worth. I think it is helpful to woodworkers to know what this plane is and how to use it.

This plane is not used to make mortises per se, but rather what is called a *gain*, that is, a shallow mortise or recess for mounting a butt hinge and the plates of other hardware. The gain is first outlined by scoring the gain to the depth of the thickness of the hinge's leaf with a chisel; then the plane clears the chips and shapes the mortise. In order to clear the chips, the mortise plane has a mouth more than an inch wide. The plane is narrow and sits comfortably on the edge of a door, unlike a router plane that is hard to balance on a narrow edge.

I often use my mortise plane when I have only a few gains to cut and making a router template would take too long. Often I can have the gains cut in the time it would take to make up the template. I also sometimes use the plane to finesse or correct the gain when the cut from a router template is a little off. To get a good fit on a door, I check the width of the gains (from the front of the door to the back) with a cutting gauge and mark any that are narrower so they are all exactly the same width. After a stop cut with a chisel, I then lift the sliver out using the mortise plane.

Whatever the style of mortise plane you have, it is important that it uses a blade mounted in the traditional bench plane manner as opposed to using a low-angle blade mounted as it would be in a router plane. This is because a blade angled only a few degrees above parallel to the sole of the plane (as in a router plane) will not have enough clearance to cut a gain that is any shorter than about twice the length of the blade, greatly reducing the versatility of the plane.

Cutting a Mortise For a Hinge Using a Mortise Plane

1 Mark the length of the hinge leaf precisely with a knife or scribe, using a square to scribe the end cut.

Cutting a Mortise For a Hinge
Using a Mortise Plane *(Continued)*

2 Scribe the width of the leaf using a cutting gauge, so that all the hinge gains will be the same and the face of the door and frame will be flush.

3 Chisel a stop cut at both ends and then a V-cut at each end of the gain to a depth equal to the thickness of the hinge leaf. If you feel insecure about judging this, you can mark the thickness of the leaf on the face of the door. The V-cuts and all successive chisel cuts do not have to be to the exact depth but rather to just less than the exact depth.

4 Cut a series of successive cuts ⅟₁₆" to ⅛" (2 to 3mm) apart and just shy of the final depth of the gain from one end to the other. If you rest your hand on the edge holding the chisel in the same position just above the surface, you can make these cuts in very rapid succession with only one or two taps of the hammer each cut.

Cutting a Mortise For a Hinge
Using a Mortise Plane *(Continued)*

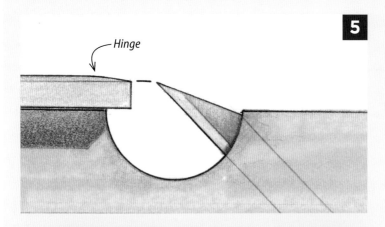

5

5 Set the blade of the mortise plane to where the aris formed by the buffing of the hardware stops. If the door is to be painted, set the depth a paper's thickness less than that.

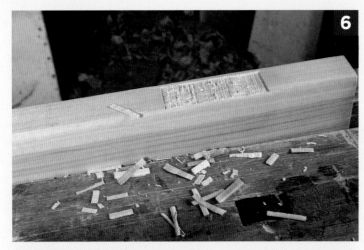

6

6 Break away any loose chips with your finger.

7

7 Run the plane over the gain, cutting away the remaining chips. It is often best to cut the full depth of the mortise in two passes: the first removing the majority of the chips cut by the chisel, not bearing down with the plane but maintaining light contact with the edge of the door; the second, after clearing away all the chips, by making full contact with the edge of the door so that the blade cuts the full depth. Cut to one end of the mortise.

Hinge

8 Then reverse the plane, cleaning the mortise to the other end.

9 Make sure you work completely to the end, all corners, and the edge.

10 Check the fit.

PART 3:
The Projects

Making a Dovetail Plane

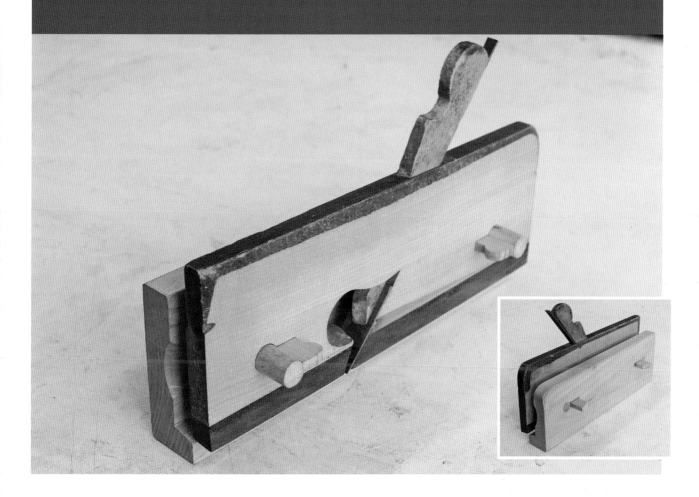

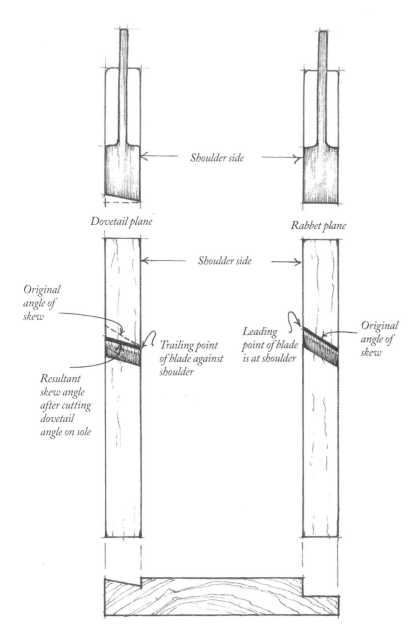

FIGURE 13-1.

Shoulder side

Dovetail plane

Rabbet plane

Shoulder side

Original angle of skew

Trailing point of blade against shoulder

Leading point of blade is at shoulder

Original angle of skew

Resultant skew angle after cutting dovetail angle on sole

Depending on the initial condition of your plane, repurposing a rabbet plane into a dovetail plane can go pretty quickly. It is a worthy reuse of a plane that has had its blade badly ground over the years and in which the angle of the edge no longer matches that of the mouth opening—which is most of them that I've seen. Making a dovetail plane requires regrinding the angle of the blade edge, which might not take much more time than it would to restore the correct angle on the original rabbet plane (assuming you don't need a rabbet plane).

Creating the Plane

The dovetail plane shown on page 131 is made from a restored traditional skewed-blade wood rabbet plane. It was badly twisted when I got it, but it was cheap and the blade was good. The misalignment of the front and back sections was bad enough that I cut them off and replaced the section as shown in **Figures 4-15A, 4-15B,** and **4-15C** on page 73. I fitted a fence to it fixed with wedges. It is particularly useful on smaller work where the E.C. Emerich would be a bit ungainly.

Start by setting up the plane as described in "Setting up Rabbet Planes" (page 65), and "Restoring a Wood Rabbet Plane" (page 74) but stop short of grinding the blade.

Once the overall block has been set up, you can cut the sole to the dovetail angle. Pick an angle, usually between 10° and 17° (I prefer the lower angles) or one that matches one of your dovetail router bits, and trim the sole of the plane to this angle. **Important**: This must be done in the correct direction (**Figure 13-1**). It is important that the trailing point of the blade be against the shouldercut of the dovetail, the opposite of the rabbet plane. This is because the dovetail plane makes a cut angled into the grain; if the lead point of the blade is against the shoulder of the cut with the blade angled back, the blade will cut up into the grain and lift and tear it (**Figure 13-2**). It's a bit hard to visualize (and harder to explain), but once you work with the plane, you will see what I mean.

This also means that when the sole is cut, the angle of skew will change to a more obtuse angle (see **Figure 13-1**). In fact, if your original skew angle and blade angle are shallow and your dovetail angle severe, you could lose your skew angle altogether.

Mark the new angle of the throat on the blade and grind the blade to match, grinding first at 90° to the edge, then grinding the bevel until the blunt grind just disappears. Test and regrind until you have a match. You may have to grind the width of the blade down to match that of the plane body; remember to maintain the relief angles on the sides of the blade. This grinding can take a while, so be patient and don't burn the blade.

Hone the blade, finish fitting it, and finish truing the sole (see **Figure 4-14**, page 72). And there you have it, a new dovetail plane. Use it as you would an unfenced rabbet plane against a

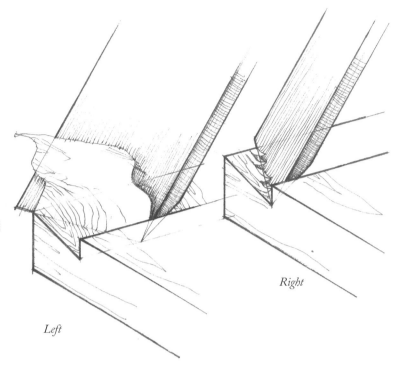

Left

Right

FIGURE 13-2. In the dovetail plane configuration (left), with the trailing point against the shoulder of the cut, the blade will shear "down" the cut. In the rabbet plane configuration (right), the trailing edge of the blade will lift the grain.

straightedge clamped to the work. If it's cross grain work, you can make knife cuts against the straightedge, or a cutting gauge to set the width and set the straightedge against this line.

Making a Fence

Adding a fence, however, certainly makes the plane more convenient to use. I made this fence out of a single piece (though, of course, it could be glued up). Its overall size was determined by the depth of cut achievable on a 10" (254mm) table saw—around 2¾" (70mm) (**Figure 13-3**). Make the cut that matches the angle of the dovetail sole first, then cut the waste free

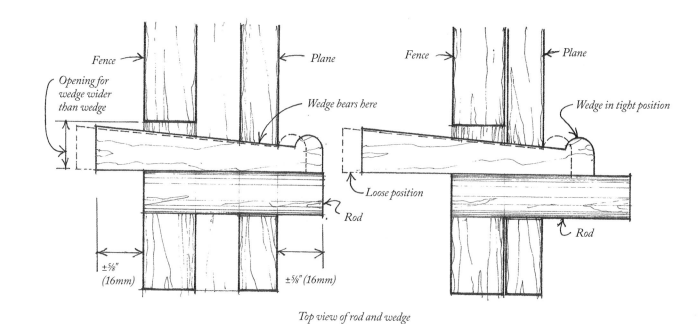

Fence

Plane

Opening for
wedge wider
than wedge

Wedge bears here

Loose position

Rod

±⅝"
(16mm)

±⅝" (16mm)

Fence

Plane

Wedge in tight position

Rod

Top view of rod and wedge

FIGURE 13-3.

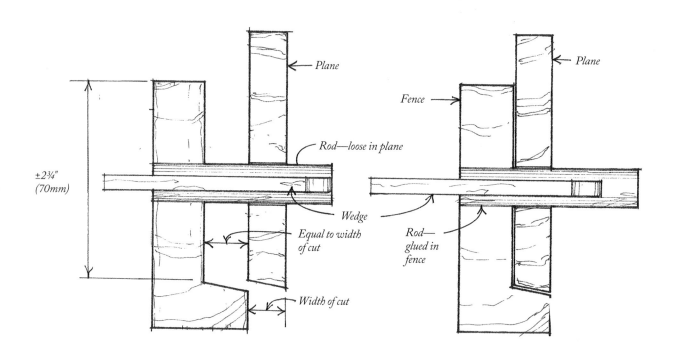

Plane

Rod—loose in plane

Wedge

Equal to width
of cut

Width of cut

±2¾"
(70mm)

Plane

Fence

Rod—
glued in
fence

End view at rod and wedge

with the deep cut. Clean up the cuts with a rabbet plane (of course!).

Using one or two business cards as spacers between the plane, fence, and foot of the fence, securely tape and/or clamp the two together (**Figure 13-4**). Mark for the dowel rods and drill their holes on a drill press (you're going to have to do this on a drill press—accuracy is required here). Make sure your dowels are accurately sized to your drill bit (do some tests) so you can get a good fit into the holes in the fence.

Securing the Fence with Wedges

The fence is locked with wedges; **Figure 13-3** shows the overall scheme. The rods are glued into the fence, and the plane moves in and out on these rods, locked into position with the wedges. The geometry of the wedges has some requirements. They have to be long enough to protrude through the backside of the fence so you can tap them to tighten them, and they have to only tighten down on the plane body. For this reason, the slot in the fence is wider than the wedges' overall width for freedom of movement. So the wedges don't go flying across the room through the fence when you tap them to loosen them, they have little nibs to restrain them. The nibs have to have enough distance between them and the plane to be able to be loosened.

Make a trial wedge that will be used to lay out their mortises and as

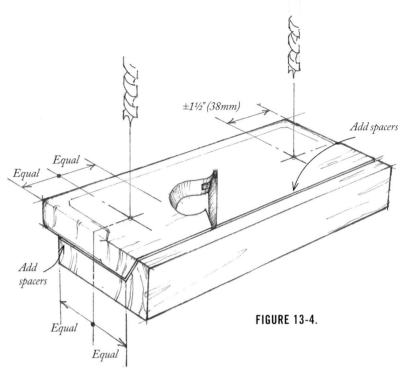

±1½" (38mm)

Add spacers

Equal
Equal
Equal

Add spacers

Equal

Equal

FIGURE 13-4.

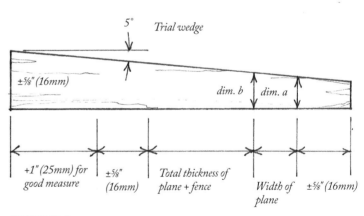

5° Trial wedge

±⅝" (16mm)

dim. b   dim. a

+1" (25mm) for good measure

±⅝" (16mm)

Total thickness of plane + fence

Width of plane

±⅝" (16mm)

FIGURE 13-5.

a template to make the final wedges (**Figure 13-5**).

Mark the thickness of the wedge, centered on the dowel. Then transfer

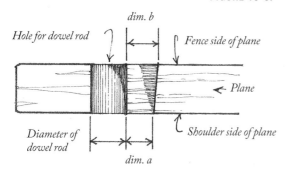

FIGURE 13-6.

Hole for dowel rod

dim. b

Fence side of plane

← Plane

Diameter of dowel rod

Shoulder side of plane

dim. a

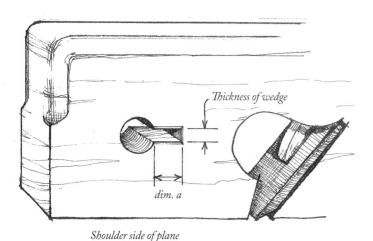

Thickness of wedge

dim. a

Shoulder side of plane

dimensions "a" and "b" of the taper onto the plane body, the narrow end of the taper ("a") at the shoulder-line side of the plane, with "b" at the fence side. Chisel this mortise and the mortise in the fence **(Figure 13-6)**.

You can see that the mortises are accurately trimmed when the edge of the trial wedge lines up with the edge of the hole at the marked lines. Once the mortises are correct, you can glue the rods into the fence. Sand the rods down a bit so that the portion that rides in the plane body is loose enough to allow free movement. Don't sand the portion that will be glued into the fence; that can be done as a final fitting after they are glued into place. While the glue dries, as a check for alignment, place the holes of the plane body over the rods and make sure everything is parallel.

When the glue has dried, you can do the final fitting of the rods and mortises. Try the trial wedge in each hole and pare the tapered mortise as required so that the wedge taps in the same distance on both rods when it locks. Note the travel it takes to loosen the wedge; this plus a little locates the nib. Make up the final wedges, using the trial as a template, and refine their fit as required. Cut some finger recesses on the ends of the fence so you can get them apart from having been pushed fully together.

14

Making and Using Shooting Boards

FIGURE 14-1. Three shooting boards: the one at the left is the down-and-dirty version with a stop block screwed to a base at the end of a piece of ¼" (6mm) tempered hardboard. The center one has a parallel ramp that allows a greater depth of cut than the one on the right, which has a sloping ramp to extend wear over a greater portion of the blade. The two boards on the right have their stops dovetailed in so that they are removable for maintenance.

FIGURE 14-2.
A quick and easy shooting board.

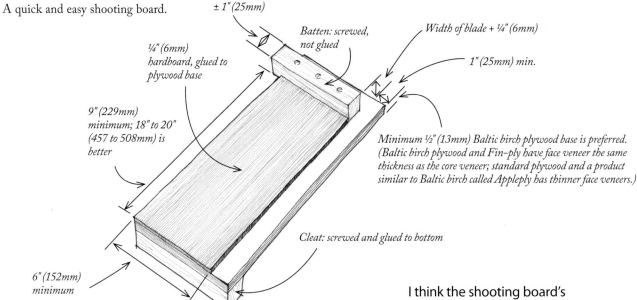

± 1" (25mm)

Batten: screwed, not glued

¼" (6mm) hardboard, glued to plywood base

Width of blade + ¼" (6mm)

1" (25mm) min.

9" (229mm) minimum; 18" to 20" (457 to 508mm) is better

Minimum ½" (13mm) Baltic birch plywood base is preferred. (Baltic birch plywood and Fin-ply have face veneer the same thickness as the core veneer; standard plywood and a product similar to Baltic birch called Appleply has thinner face veneers.)

Cleat: screwed and glued to bottom

6" (152mm) minimum

Probably the single most effective accessory for any bench is the shooting board, or its cousin the bench hook (**Figure 14-1**). I underestimated the usefulness of this tool for a long time, but have gradually become more and more appreciative of its speed and versatility. Its first use is the trimming of ends of pieces, either square (probably most useful) or at a particular angle, such as 45°, done on a shooting board made just for this angle. Using a shooting board for trimming can greatly increase your accuracy. You can take off the thickness of a shaving, say a few thousandths of an inch, with each stroke, giving you incredible accuracy. Because the stop supports the grain at the back of the strip, you do not have to worry about your piece chipping out at the exit side of the cut.

I think the shooting board's usefulness is finally becoming appreciated, and you can now find a large number of designs. The great thing is you can customize this tool to suit the kind of work you do: large work, small work, veneer, specific repeated pieces, specific angles—and have several of them as needed.

Designing a Shooting Board

Here are a few things to think about when designing your shooting board:

- **Maximize your cut.** A lot of shooting boards have a ½" (13mm) or thicker base the work sits on. As the side of the plane at the blade opening that registers against this base is rarely more than ¼" (6mm) wide, you're losing ¼" (6mm) of cutting capacity. Likewise, the stop should be as high as your blade is wide. Though paring the ends of boards this thick (especially if you like to use a #7 or #8 Stanley jointer) is not something most workers do often, it does allow you to shim thinner pieces of work up to utilize that higher part of the blade that often goes unused.

- If you're trimming a lot of thin work, **slope the ramp**. This extends the area of wear, because if you repeatedly trim very narrow hardwood, say ⅛" (3mm) or less, after a dozen strokes that ⅛" (3mm) of your blade will be dull—sometimes virtually dented. This will require a lot of sharpening of an otherwise still-sharp plane.

- Additionally, have some **boards of different thicknesses** on hand to be used as shims when planing a series of thin pieces. The boards can move the work up and down to unused areas of the blade. You can extend the wear all over your blade this way, vastly shortening the amount of time you need to sharpen.

- **The stop must be adjustable and replaceable.** A screwed and glued stop will eventually shift its adjustment (yes, I know it's magic, but it happens), though usually not before the end wears out. This necessitates ripping the old one out and probably making a new board. A stop using a screw-tightening device to hold its adjustment will definitely shift. Besides being able to periodically refine the squareness of the stop, the length of it should be adjustable to present a fresh end to support the work and keep it from splintering out.

Styles of Shooting Boards

There are two styles of shooting boards: one that runs parallel to the length of the bench (i.e., left and right), and one that runs across the bench, bench hook style.

The shooting board that runs parallel to the length of the bench is a traditional position often used for shooting sheets of veneer and the edges of intermediate length boards (with a square edge on your jointer plane). In this style the plane is used on the far side of the shooting board. Ends, of course, can be smoothed and squared, but if the boards are very long, you'll need to support the piece using a separate supporting device such as an adjustable horse.

A bench hook style of shooting board that goes across the bench is more limited in the length of the edge (width of the board) it can trim: roughly the width of your bench—or the length of your reach, maybe 24" to 30" (610 to 760mm). However, it can more easily trim the ends of boards of almost any length (unlike the other style of shooting board). It does this simply by keeping a spare piece of wood around the same thickness as the bed of your shooting board to use as a shim to prop up the piece.

If you're using a bench hook type of shooting board where a batten on the underside catches on the front edge of the bench, you can use that batten as a planing stop by turning the board over. Make that stop thinner so you can plane thinner pieces of wood, such as drawer sides. This style of shooting board is very effective for drawer work: you can face plane drawer pieces, plane the height of the sides to exactly fit your pocket, and the length of all pieces to an exact fit, without having to clamp or unclamp anything.

A shooting board made at a 45° angle is also useful—indispensable, really—if you are doing miters such as the ends of stops for holding panels or glass within the stiles and rails of a door (**Figure 14-3**). A shooting board for 45° trimming was my first shooting board, actually. Years ago, I was trying to fit many stops on several glass doors for a cabinet. Despite setting up consistent jigs for cutting the different lengths, quite a number of the stops still needed finessing, resulting in much frustration and lost time.

Later, I mentioned this problem to my uncle, who was a patternmaker, and he sent back a drawing of a shooting board for trimming miters, a device he had used for many years. The drawing was enlightening (**Figure 14-4**). This tool makes trimming pieces to exact length easy and safe. Additionally, unlike the single stop versions, I found that my uncle's design, with its double miter, is ideally suited for moldings as well as flat pieces, because some moldings can't be flipped against the stop and still register properly to do both right and left miters. While this stop cannot be adjusted, I found that in much work the angle may have to be tweaked a half a degree or so anyway to pull up nicely. This custom angle is easily accomplished (especially if it is more acute) by actually holding the piece slightly off the far side of the stop, or shimming it at an increased angle with a stray shaving or two stuck behind it. (An obtuse angle is more difficult, as shimming the piece at the working end of the stop risks blowing out the back side of the piece because it is not supported.)

FIGURE 14-3. A 45° shooting board is indispensable for fine miter work.

FIGURE 14-4. A shooting board for miters. (Construction is similiar to **Figure 14-2** on page 138.)

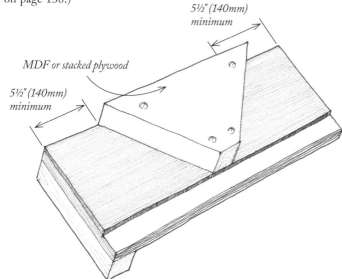

5½" (140mm) minimum

MDF or stacked plywood

5½" (140mm) minimum

Additionally, versions can be made for trimming any angle, say parts for a hexagon. They are often worth the time it takes if you have many joints to trim.

Another joint that often needs trimming is the face miter, that is, a miter cut across the width of the board at the end of a 1 by 4 or 1 by 6, for instance, as might be found in a fascia or baseboard of a cabinet. This mitered end is wider than the plane blade and thus can't be used with the shooting board previously described. Traditionally, variations of a device often called a donkey's ear, miter jack, or miter shooting block were used to help shoot this joint. To me, these always looked to be awkward to use, elaborate to make, and expensive to buy—when you could find them.

When using the donkey's ear, because the work is held at an angle to the floor, the length of the piece to be trimmed is limited by the working height off the floor. Eventually, I figured out a simplified version of the traditional shooting board to trim these miters (**Figure 14-5**). Moreover, because it functions similarly to the classic shooting board, the length of the piece to be trimmed is not limited (you might have a piece for a built-in that is 12′–16′ [3.6–4.8m] long). Basically, it is a shooting board with the ledge at 45° to the surface upon which the work rests. The edge of this surface and the stop are cut at a complimentary 45° to back up the plane cut. I've since made a couple more shooting boards of this style at different angles (**Figures 14-6** and **14-7**).

FIGURE 14-5. This shooting board is for trimming face miters: a 45° angle cut across the grain of wide boards.

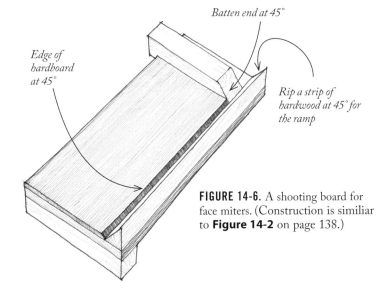

Edge of hardboard at 45°

Batten end at 45°

Rip a strip of hardwood at 45° for the ramp

FIGURE 14-6. A shooting board for face miters. (Construction is similiar to **Figure 14-2** on page 138.)

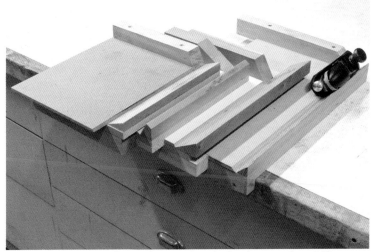

FIGURE 14-7. Four different shooting boards for shooting four different angles of face miters, each made for a specific project.

Using a Shooting Board

You can use any plane on a shooting board, except a rabbet plane, as a rabbet plane will continually cut into the ledge on which it rides. Lower-angle planes—ones with a 45° cutting (blade) angle or less—will work better for cutting end grain. The low-angle Stanley-style block plane is a good candidate, although many woodworkers prefer one of the larger bench planes. The low-angle jack and smoothing planes are also good choices. In addition, some planes were made specifically for miter or shooting-board work (called, coincidentally, *miter planes*). And a special wood plane was sometimes used, fitted with an iron plate at the throat for wear, a skewed blade for a shearing cut, and a handle to hook your hand around mounted at an angle to the work. At one time Stanley made an iron version of this plane, the #51 that went with its own iron shooting/miter board; this has since been brought back to life with both Lie-Nielsen and Lee Valley producing their own versions.

Currently I am experimenting with using the Lee Valley skewed-blade block plane. With its angled blade, it functions similarly to the old skewed-blade miter plane, shearing the grain at an angle, reducing the effort needed.

Heft or extra length is not necessary in a plane used on the shooting board. The use of a heavy plane encourages getting a "running start" with the plane. The main requirements are

- keep the blade sharp—and sharpened straight with no curve and adjusted parallel to the sole;

- square the sole to the side that runs on the ledge; and

- cut lightly with the plane.

In use, the plane touches the workpiece, and the user pushes it the length of the cut to shear a shaving off. Many first-time users make the mistake of having the blade adjusted too far out, causing the plane to stall in the cut.

The common reaction is to get a running start with the plane and crash it into the piece. Don't. It is hard on the plane (and you) and results in inaccurate work. Adjust the plane for a light cut. If the plane does not seem to be cutting, make sure the end of the piece is projecting a fraction past the stop. The plane may cut only a tiny piece of the corner at first, but will gradually extend the cut. You should be able to shear the shaving off in a smooth push. Admittedly, however, some cuts will require a bit of momentum.

FIGURE 14-8. A shooting board solves all the problems of planing an end-grain edge. You can quickly and easily plane virtually any size board, producing a perfectly straight, square, splinter-free, and consistent-looking edge, not to mention continuous transparent shavings—but only if the plane is properly sharpened and set.

The Dovetailed Stop

I first designed this board as a class project for woodworking classes I was teaching at the time. While I thought then that it was a bit of overkill to dovetail the stops into the boards, I also thought it was a good demonstration of the use of a number of different joinery planes: rabbet, side-rabbet, dovetail, and router (and possibly dado) planes, as well a number of techniques with a smoothing plane.

I'm still using the first one I made over 20 years ago and have yet had to replace the stop, though of course I've had to trim and square it up on occasion. I certainly like it better than a collection of plywood and screws sitting on my bench.

To solve the problem of having to periodically replace the stop, this shooting board uses a stop that is fixed to the board with a tapering, single-sided sliding dovetail friction-fit into place. This piece has extra length so it can be removed, the working face squared up if it needs to be (without affecting the fit), and the stop tapped back into place. The end of the stop can often be renewed by tapping the stop further out a little bit, then planing the end clean with the plane you use to shoot. While after doing this a few times the stop becomes fully compressed and must be tapped back out, a shaving can then be taken off the back of it to reduce its width. This will allow it to advance in the cut, and then it can be tapped back into a position where it can be trimmed.

FIGURE 14-9. My two most-used shooting boards. They have seen use nearly every working day for 20 years. Though the stops have been re-tuned several times, they have yet to be replaced. The longer board on the left is particularly good for drawer parts as I can also flip it over and face plane against the thinner stop on the bottom.

Bench Hook Versus Shooting Board

A bench hook is almost identical to the shooting board. The differences are the bench hook does not have a ramp (also called a ledge, or rebate), it tends to be shorter than a shooting board, and it is used mostly as a saw stop, though it can also be used for shooting edges and ends. The shooting board usually has a ramp, can be as long as needed when used to shoot edges, and is primarily used for planing ends and edges, though it, as well, can be used as a saw stop.

In order to extend the wear across a wider portion of the blade and the time between sharpenings, and simultaneously reduce blade wear on the one narrow portion of the blade that happens as a result of a running the plane on a parallel ledge, especially with thin stock, I cut the ledge as a long tapering rabbet, creating a ramp for the plane to ride on.

Making a Shooting Board

1&2 There are two forms of the standard 90° shooting board. The first **(Image 1)** has a parallel ramp for the plane, which allows for planing thick pieces of wood. The second **(Image 2)** has a sloping ramp. While the slope reduces the thickness of the pieces of wood it handles, the blade wear spreads across a wider area.

3&4 Prepare stock for your shooting board. For the base, use a piece at least 7" wide by 12" to 24" long (178mm by 305mm to 610mm). The shorter length is a little more convenient to move around and store. The longer length allows you to do wider and longer pieces, such as drawer parts, but puts you working at the far side of the bench because the stop is 20"+ (508mm+) away from you. Do not make the shooting board longer than your bench is wide. Use any species of wood as long as it is dry and has stopped moving, though using rift or quartersawn stock provides the best stability.

For the parallel-ledge version, the board needs to be at least ¾" (19mm) thick. For the sloping ramp version, it should be at least 1" (25mm) thick. Determine the cross-sectional dimensions of the stops, or battens, from the information in **Images 3** and **4**. Mill these

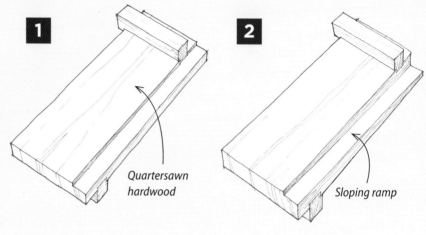

Quartersawn hardwood

Sloping ramp

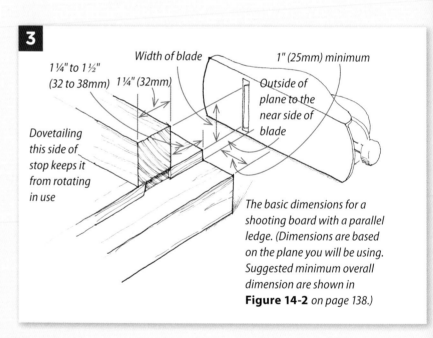

1¼" to 1½" (32 to 38mm)   1¼" (32mm)

Width of blade   1" (25mm) minimum

Dovetailing this side of stop keeps it from rotating in use

Outside of plane to the near side of blade

The basic dimensions for a shooting board with a parallel ledge. (Dimensions are based on the plane you will be using. Suggested minimum overall dimension are shown in **Figure 14-2** on page 138.)

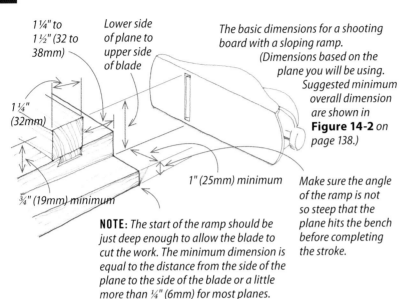

1¼" to 1½" (32 to 38mm)

Lower side of plane to upper side of blade

1¼" (32mm)

¾" (19mm) minimum

1" (25mm) minimum

The basic dimensions for a shooting board with a sloping ramp. (Dimensions based on the plane you will be using. Suggested minimum overall dimension are shown in **Figure 14-2** *on page 138.)*

Make sure the angle of the ramp is not so steep that the plane hits the bench before completing the stroke.

NOTE: *The start of the ramp should be just deep enough to allow the blade to cut the work. The minimum dimension is equal to the distance from the side of the plane to the side of the blade or a little more than ¼" (6mm) for most planes.*

and cut them 2" or 3" (51 or 76mm) longer than the board is wide. This will give you extra length to correct the fit if needed and to re-pair the end of the stop as it wears over time. It also does not hurt to make an extra one or two of these.

The shooting boards shown are for right-handers. If you are left-handed, you will probably want the ledge or ramp on the left. If you want to use a pull plane—and are right-handed—you will also want a left-handed ramp, though you will use the shooting board with the ramp on the right, the board hooked over the far side of the bench.

5

NOTES:

- *Always reference off one face and one edge that you are sure are straight, flat, and square to each other. The reference edge should also be the edge upon which the ramp will be formed.*

- *The narrow end of the tapered dovetail is at the ramp side. The taper allows you to cut off and clean up the end of a stop that has been worn over time and then plane a stroke or two (literally) off the back of the stop to advance it to the correct position when it is tapped back into place.*

- *In laying out the dovetails, some lines are cut lines, and some lines are layout lines used to derive the cut lines. It is helpful (and more accurate) to use a scribe or marking knife for the cut lines, and pencil for the layout (non-cut) lines. Pencil allows you to erase the layout lines for correction or for clarity.*

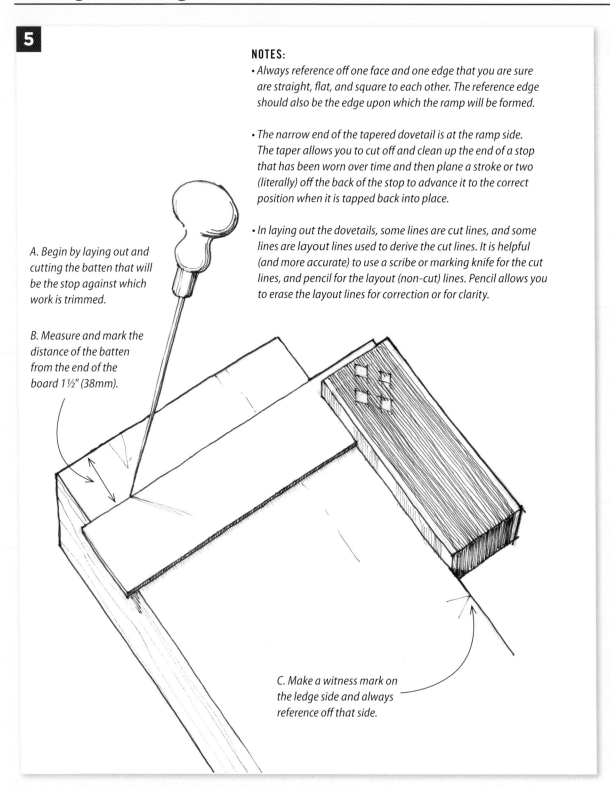

A. Begin by laying out and cutting the batten that will be the stop against which work is trimmed.

B. Measure and mark the distance of the batten from the end of the board 1½" (38mm).

C. Make a witness mark on the ledge side and always reference off that side.

6 Place the batten on the marked line and carefully mark the width. Err on the side of narrower.

7 Mark the batten width precisely with a sharp pencil.

8 Continue the marks around the edges of the board. They need not extend all the way across the edges. Continue the pencil mark.

9 Mark the depth of the dovetail—about ¼" (6mm), or the same as the step-down of the ledge, if you are making a parallel ledge.

10 Take a bevel gauge and set it to the angle of your dovetail plane.

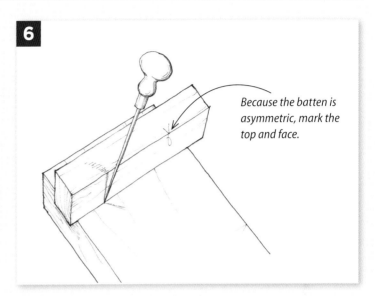

Because the batten is asymmetric, mark the top and face.

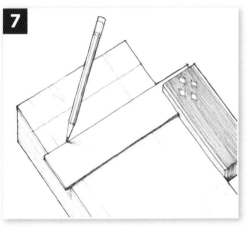

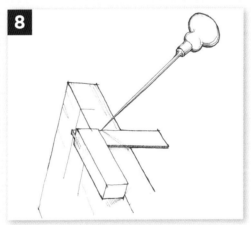

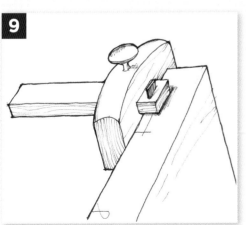

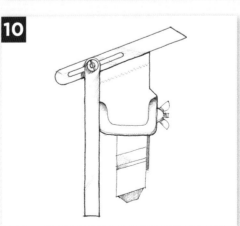

Making a Shooting Board *(Continued)*

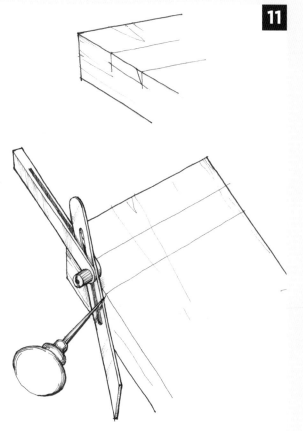

11 Transfer the angle you measured in step 10 to the edge of the board at the precise intersection of the mark for the bottom of the dovetail (marking gauge line) and the width of the batten (pencil line). Err on the side of a narrower dovetail.

12 Mark a line (in pencil) square across the face of the board connected to the dovetail angle line.

13 Make a mark on the ramp side ⅛" (3mm) up from the pencil line. With a straightedge, scribe a line from the dovetail mark on the edge opposite the ramp side to the ⅛" (3mm) mark on the ramp side. This is the taper of the dovetail. (Note: The amount of taper is not critical. However, if you have too much, the batten knocks loose easily. If you have too little, the requirements for matching the angle of the taper exactly, and its width, escalate geometrically.)

14 Mark the dovetail angle on the edge of the board from the taper line on the face.

15 Make up a guide block at least as long as the width of the board (if you make it longer, you can use it for other projects later). The guide block should be at least 1" (25mm) thick, with one edge ripped square, the other at the angle of the dovetail (the same angle as your dovetail plane). Clamp

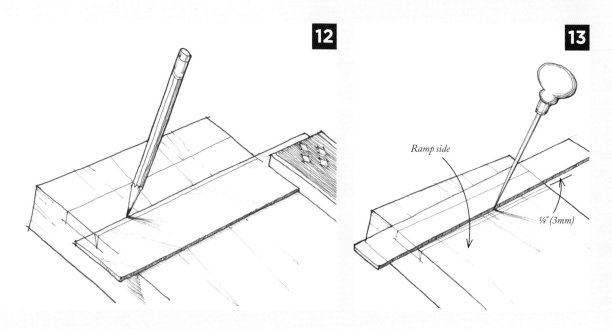

Ramp side

⅛" (3mm)

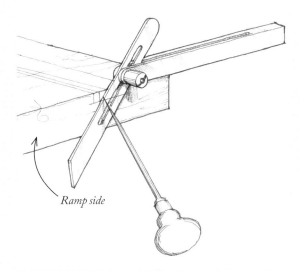

14

Ramp side

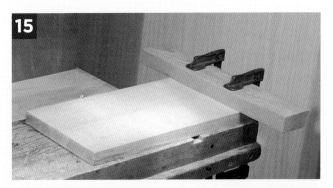

15

the edge of the guide precisely on the scribe line, and to the outside of what will be the dovetail groove, so that you will be cutting into the waste. Use the square edge of the guide on the cut toward the end of the board, because this cut is square.

16

16. Using a Japanese *ázebiki* (mortise) saw in contact with the guide, make a sawcut the full depth of the groove as marked, square to the surface of the board, and extending the full width of the board. Normally, the crosscut teeth are used, as this cut is across the grain. Sometimes, however, if the teeth load too fast, it may be preferable to use the rip teeth. Stop frequently to clear the gullets of the saw. To improve accuracy, keep a light pressure on the saw against the guide with your other hand. The *ázebiki* saw is ideally suited for this job. You can use a Western back saw that's big enough to clear every-thing, but I think you will find the shallower teeth of the back saw load quicker; it is harder to keep the full length of the back saw's blade on the guide block. You can use a sliding dovetail saw, also called a stairbuilders saw, but I find it is difficult to be ac-curate with it, and the results are rough.

17

17. Reclamp for the second cut, using the dovetail-angle side of the guide. Set the guide precisely on the scribed taper line, with the angle of its edge oriented the same as the marked flair of the dovetail. Cut into the *waste side* of the scribed line, to the full depth of the cut, and extending the full width of the board. Make a clean start (very important) by keeping pres-sure against the guide board.

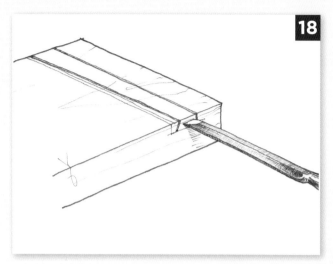

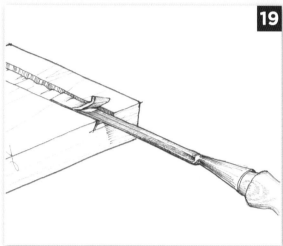

18 Clear most of the waste with a chisel, taking small amounts at a time to avoid breaking out the wood below the scribe line on the edge of the board.

19 Work in from both sides to avoid splitting out at the ends.

20 Clear the waste to within about 1/16" (2mm) of the bottom. Carefully pare in from each end down to the scribed depth line for about 3/4" (19mm) from the edge of the board into the groove.

21 Adjust the router plane to just take the high spots off the remaining waste. Clean the waste, and then lower the blade and shave away more waste. Continue until the bottom of the groove is completely level and at the precise depth of the scribe line.

22 Inspect the groove. Sight down it to see if the sides are straight. Check also that the bottom corners are clean. Clean these up if required.

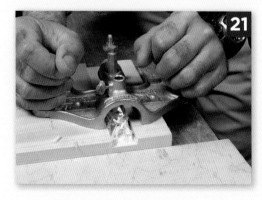

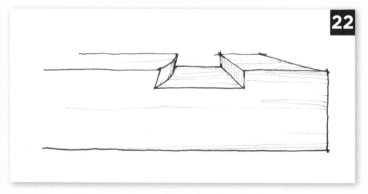

23

A. Use a side-rabbet plane to straighten up sides that are uneven or curved. While you can use a Japanese-style side rabbet plane as shown here, the Stanley-style side rabbet plane is effective also. (See Chapter 10 on page 116.)

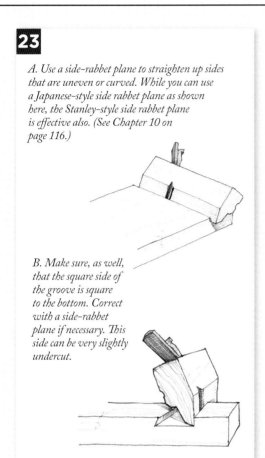

B. Make sure, as well, that the square side of the groove is square to the bottom. Correct with a side-rabbet plane if necessary. This side can be very slightly undercut.

24

B. Then mark the taper, starting at the mark for the board width, tapering toward the ramp end of the batten. This can be marked in pencil.

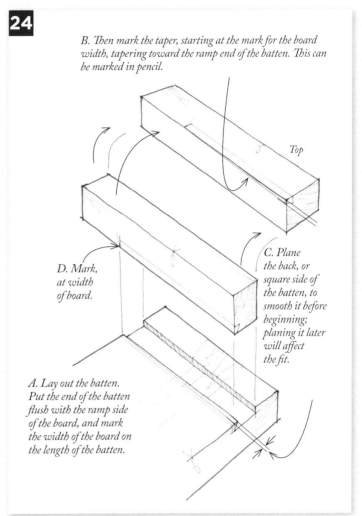

Top

C. Plane the back, or square side of the batten, to smooth it before beginning; planing it later will affect the fit.

D. Mark, at width of board.

A. Lay out the batten. Put the end of the batten flush with the ramp side of the board, and mark the width of the board on the length of the batten.

25

A. Set the fence on the dovetail plane using the marking gauge that was used to mark the depth of the groove. If the depth of the groove was overshot, reset the marking gauge to the new depth.

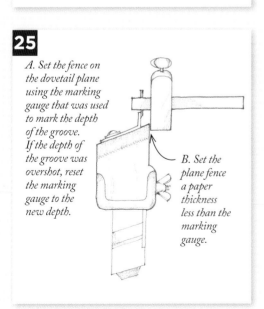

B. Set the plane fence a paper thickness less than the marking gauge.

26

$\leq \frac{1}{64}"$ (0.4mm)

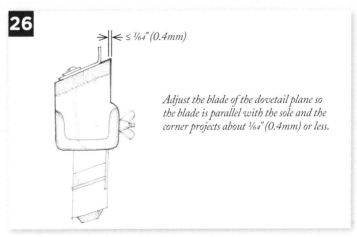

Adjust the blade of the dovetail plane so the blade is parallel with the sole and the corner projects about 1/64" (0.4mm) or less.

Making a Shooting Board *(Continued)*

27 Clamp the batten in a vise or a handscrew clamp clamped to the bench, so it projects enough for the plane's fence to clear. With the plane held vertical (that is, not tilted) and the fence against the batten, make a short stroke at the narrow end of the tapered dovetail. Make repeated short strokes to establish a cut parallel to the marked taper line.

28 Once the cut is established parallel to the marked taper line, make precise full stokes of the plane to lengthen the cut until it is within about 1⁄16" (2mm) of the line and parallel to it.

29 Tap the batten in until it stops moving. Pull up at the front and then at the back of the batten. If it lifts at the front, the taper is too narrow there. If it lifts at the back, it is too narrow there. Visually inspect the joint as well. If the joint taps in tight but shows gaps at both ends, either the batten tenon or the groove is curved, or both are. Remove the batten by tapping it back out and sight down the parts to determine what to adjust. Correct a curve in the length of the groove with a side rabbet plane. Correct a curve in the length of the tenon with the dovetail plane. Note: Except for correcting for straight, no work is done on the groove when fitting the dovetail of the batten. Do all work on the batten with the dovetail plane.

30 Put the batten back in the vise and plane the dovetail, gradually extending the cut until it runs the full length. Take no more than three or four strokes before checking the fit. If your taper matched that of the groove, take full-length strokes from the batten, trying to maintain parallel.

31 If the dovetail plane was miss-set, correct the steps with the side rabbet plane.

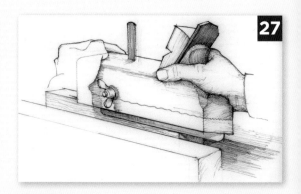

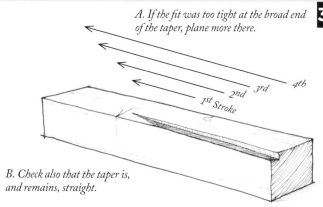

A. If the fit was too tight at the broad end of the taper, plane more there.

4th

3rd

2nd

1st Stroke

B. Check also that the taper is, and remains, straight.

C. Because of the geometry, each shaving advances the batten in its slot quite a bit. A heavy shaving could advance the batten almost 1⁄8" (3mm) or more. So check the fit every 3 or 4 strokes—or less. When you are within about an inch of the end, check every 2 or 3 strokes. Make sure, however, on each trial that the taper is parallel by lifting the ends.

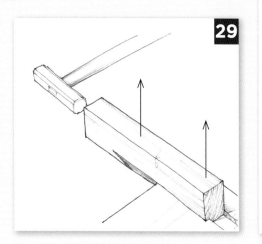

32 At each trial fit, use a small hammer or mallet to lightly tap the batten into place. (Remember to keep a strong downward pressure on the batten with your other hand as you tap it in to keep it from riding up). Stop when the batten stops moving. When it is snug just at the far edge of the board, you are done. If you overshoot it—that is why the batten is overlong—you can trim it to fit. If, however, you run out of length, you will have to make another batten. Next, flip the board over and fit the other batten. This second batten will be on the underside and will hook against the front edge of the bench or work surface in use, keeping the board from scooting across the bench. It can also be placed in the front vise to hold it even more securely.

33 To cut the ledge upon which the plane will run, set up the fillister-plane fence to an inch or more from the side of the plane. Set the blade parallel to the sole, projecting out the side about 1/64" (0.4mm) or less. If you are making a shooting board with a parallel ledge, you can cut the ledge with a table saw or router. It can be cleaned up with the rabbet plane. If you are making a shooting board with a sloping ramp, it is surprisingly fast to cut it with a fillister plane, especially when you start trying to figure out the jigging required to make the cut with a power tool—it is safer and quieter, too. It is a bit of vigorous work, but you can make this cut in less than five minutes. I know you have already spent that amount of time trying to figure out how to jig the cut for a power tool.

34 To plane the sloping ramp, remove the battens from the board. Begin at the face-batten end to establish the angle of the ramp. Work back from this end, gradually lengthening the stroke. Try to keep the ramp face, from rabbet edge to board edge, parallel to the face of the board.

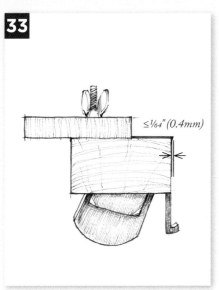

≤1/64" (0.4mm)

Making a Shooting Board *(Continued)*

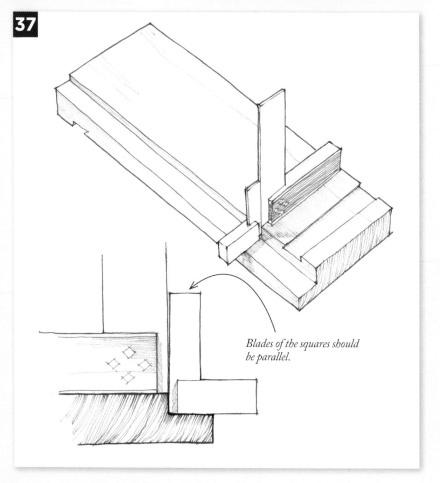

35 Ideally, your plane should be able to cut down the ramp rather than up, as shown here. This should reduce the chance of tearout. However, I have only one fillister plane, and usually experience no problem using it uphill, into the grain, when necessary.

36 The ramp angle completed.

37 When the angle of the ramp is complete, check the surface for parallel to the face of the board by putting a square on each surface and seeing if the blades are parallel. Check every 3" or 4" (76 or 102mm) along the length. Reset the fillister plane to a finer depth of cut and correct the ramp, section by section, if necessary. End by taking one long finishing stroke with the plane.

Blades of the squares should be parallel.

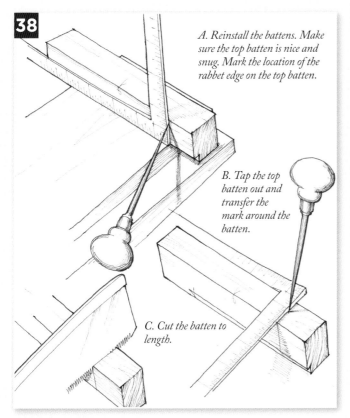

38

A. Reinstall the battens. Make sure the top batten is nice and snug. Mark the location of the rabbet edge on the top batten.

B. Tap the top batten out and transfer the mark around the batten.

C. Cut the batten to length.

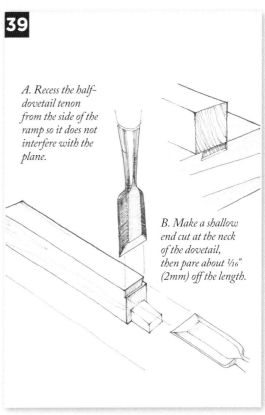

39

A. Recess the half-dovetail tenon from the side of the ramp so it does not interfere with the plane.

B. Make a shallow end cut at the neck of the dovetail, then pare about 1/16" (2mm) off the length.

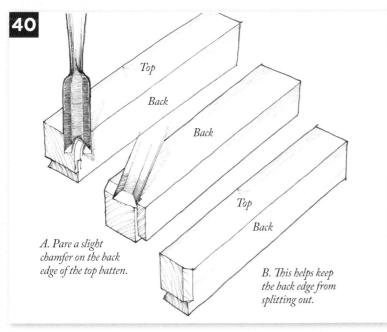

40

Top

Back

Back

Top

Back

A. Pare a slight chamfer on the back edge of the top batten.

B. This helps keep the back edge from splitting out.

38–40 Follow the instructions within images 38 to 40.

Making a Shooting Board *(Continued)*

41

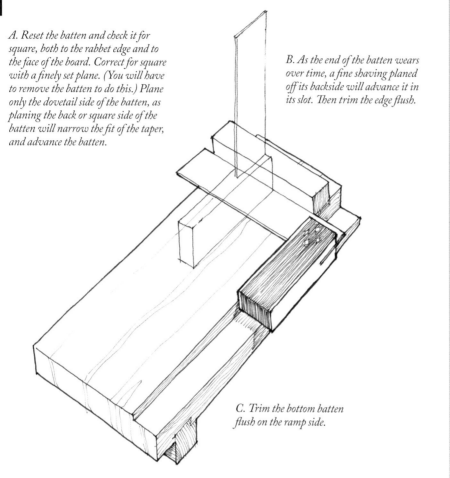

A. Reset the batten and check it for square, both to the rabbet edge and to the face of the board. Correct for square with a finely set plane. (You will have to remove the batten to do this.) Plane only the dovetail side of the batten, as planing the back or square side of the batten will narrow the fit of the taper, and advance the batten.

B. As the end of the batten wears over time, a fine shaving planed off its backside will advance it in its slot. Then trim the edge flush.

C. Trim the bottom batten flush on the ramp side.

42 The completed shooting board. A shooting board with a tapering ramp spreads the wear on the blade from trimming thin stock over a greater area, extending time between sharpenings.

INDEX

A

alloy ingredients, 17

alloyed steel, 11, 16, 19–20

anatomy of steel, 10–16

angle
    bevel angle, 23, 29–30
    of blades, 24–26, 133

annealing, 13

austenite phase, 13

B

bar stock, 12

bed, blades, 42–47, 68

bench hooks, 139, 143

bevel angle, 23, 29–30

bevel-down metal planes, 44–45

bevel-up metal planes, 45–46

blade projection, 66

blade-adjustment nib, 44

blades
    angle of, 24–26, 133
    bed, 42–47, 68
    flattening the back, 37–39
    preparing, 35–36, 67–68
    tactics, 23–31
    waterstones, 40–41
    width of, 30–31

block planes, 56–57

bridge board, 115

bullnose planes, 100–102

C

carbide, 13

carbon, 17

carbon steel, 16, 18

carborundum method, 38–39

Carriage Maker's Rabbet Plane, 56, 58

cast steel blade, 16

China markers, 46

chipbreakers
    described, 23
    preparing, 41–42, 68
    use of, 28–29

chisel planes, 100–102

chrome vanadium blade, 21

chromium, 17

Clifton planes, 58–59, 96, 97, 99–101

combination planes, 93

cryogenically treated blades, 21

cutting edge
    angle of, 24–26
    ideal edge, 11
    importance of, 9
    shape of, 23, 30
    types of, 16–21
    wood species and, 24–26

cutting spur, 84, 88

D

dado planes, 55, 92–95

depth gauge rod, 107

depth stops, 84, 88

Discovering Japanese Handplanes, 57, 119

donkey's ear, 141

dovetail planes
    chrome vanadium blade, 21
    creating the plane, 132–133
    described, 120–123
    fence, making, 133–135
    fence, securing with wedges, 135–136
    repurposing a rabbet plane, 132

drop forging, 12

E

E.C. Emerich (ECE) fillister planes, 59, 85, 86, 87, 132

end grain, cutting, 23

F

fence solutions, 86–87, 133–136

fillister planes
    choosing, 85
    history of, 83–84
    rabbet plane versus, 53
    setting up, 87–88

using, 84–85, 88–90

forging, 11–12

freehand rabbet cutting, 62–64

full-length stops, 84

G

Getting Started with Handplanes, 71

grain, steel, 10–11

grain direction, 89

grain size chart, 10

H

hammer forging, 12

hardening, 13

hardness, steel, 12–16

hinges, using a mortise plane, 126–129

H.N.T. Gordon Company, 59

hollow grinding, 31

hot work, 11

I

inclusions, 10

J

joinery plane edge, 30

joint-forming plane, 84

L

Lee Valley planes
  fillister planes, 85, 86, 89
  miter planes, 142
  rabbet planes, 56–57

Lie-Nielsen planes
  bench planes, 56–58
  end grain, cutting, 23
  miter planes, 142
  router planes, 113–114
  shoulder planes, 96, 97
  side-rabbet planes, 117, 118

limiter rod, 107

M

manganese, 17

marking, 46

martensite, 13

metal planes
  bevel-down, 44–45
  bevel-up, 45–46
  inspecting, 33
  sole, configuring, 49

miter planes, 142

miter work, 140–141

mortise planes, 124–129

mouth opening
  adjusting, 50, 73
  clearance of, 23
  controlling shaving, 26–27
  going out of parallel, 43

moving-fillister plane. *See* fillister planes

N

new wood planes, inspecting, 35

nicker, 84, 88

O

old (antique) wood planes, inspecting, 33–35

P

pencil lead, 46

pitch angles, 24

plane inspections, 65

plane length, 30–31

plough planes, 26–27, 92–95

Primus planes, 59

R

rabbet bench, 56–57

rabbet plane blade, 16

rabbet planes
  basics, 54–55
  restoring, 74–81
  selection of, 59–61
  setting up, 65–74
  skewed-blade, 57–58

Stanley, 56, 58–59
term usage, 53
using, 61–64
Record planes, 58–59, 93, 97, 105
Rockwell hardness scales, 14–15
router planes
described, 103–105
other plane options, 113–114
stair stringers project, 107–112
Stanley planes, 104–106, 113
supplemental sole, 114
using, 113, 115

S

sash-fillister plane, 89
scoring knife, 84, 88
shooting boards
bench hook versus, 143
designing, 138–139
dovetailed stop, 143
making, 144–156
measurements, 138
styles, 137, 139–141
using, 142
shoulder planes, 96–99
shouldered blade, 55
side-rabbet planes, 116–119
silicon, 17
skewed-blade rabbet planes, 57–58, 69–71
sliding-dovetail, 121–122
sole
checking, 49–50
configuring, 47–49, 68, 72–73
shavings, removing, 74
supplemental, 114
square, checking for, 33
stair stringers project, 107–112
Stanley planes
combination planes, 93
end grain, cutting, 23
fence solutions, 87
fillister planes, 85
miter planes, 142
rabbet planes, 56, 57–59
router planes, 104–106, 113

shoulder planes, 97–98
side-rabbet planes, 116–119
Stanley-style block plane, 142
straightness, gauging, 48
structure, steel, 11–12

T

tactics, planes, 23
tempering, 13
tenon shoulders, 97
3-in-1 plane, 58–59, 97, 100–101
tread and riser housings, 107–112
tungsten, 17

V

V cuts, 61
Veritas planes
blades, 9
combination planes, 93
end grain, cutting, 23
fillister planes, 86
rabbet planes, 56, 57
router planes, 113–114
shoulder planes, 97
side-rabbet plane, 118

W

waterstones, 40–41
wax pencils, 46
wedges, 34, 135–136
wood planes
inspecting, 33–35, 46–47
restoring, 74–81
wood species, cutting angle and, 24–26

More Great Woodworking Books
from Fox Chapel Publishing

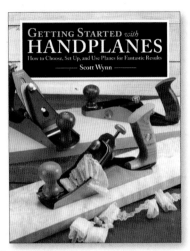
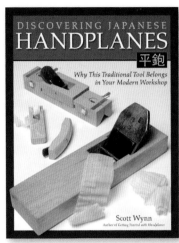

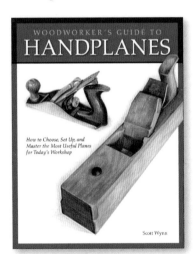
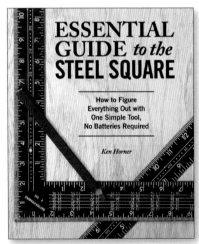
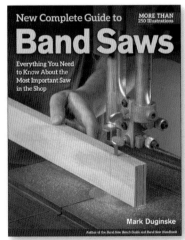